50p

KV-620-949

ON MY WAVELENGTH

ON MY WAVELENGTH

Howard Lockhart

✧✧✧

IMPULSE BOOKS

ABERDEEN

First published in 1973 by
Impulse Publications Limited
28 Guild Street
Aberdeen
Scotland

SBN 901311 33 2

© Howard Lockhart 1973

Printed in Scotland by Holmes McDougall Ltd., Aberdeen.

CONTENTS

CHAPTER 1

5SC CALLING

I USED to wonder why they called it wireless. It seemed then to be all wire, yards and yards of it. I can well remember the very first time I 'listened in'. My Ayr Academy School chum had invited me to his home to experiment with this new thing people were beginning to talk about, called 'the wireless'. Of course you didn't just turn a knob or press a button, expecting results. Oh no! Listening-in was a hobby that you worked at, rather like stamp-collecting or fretwork. There we sat, earphones clamped tightly to our heads. And, wonder of wonders, we could actually hear voices. All the way from Glasgow to Ayr, and no wires! 'Auntie Cyclone', 'Uncle Mungo' and 'Uncle Alec', singing, telling stories, or exchanging jokes and riddles in the simplest, most unpretentious manner, and we loved them.

Two years earlier, I had won a prize in a story competition in a popular children's magazine of the time, called 'Little Folks'. Would there be any chance, I wondered, of having it read, over the wireless? One Saturday, with knees well scrubbed, and wearing my Sunday suit, I was taken along Bath Street to the BBC's first studios in Glasgow. I can remember hearing Auntie's familiar voice before she came into the waiting-room, and my surprise at her appearance. The Auntie Cyclone I knew was small, dark and plump, to my way of thinking. This lady was slender, with lots of fair hair, done in the fashionable earphone style. I expect I was tongue-tied, but she had the charm to make one feel immediately at ease. She took the copy of my story from my doubtless sticky hand, glanced over it, and then announced that, if there was time, I could read it myself in the Children's Corner that very afternoon.

And thus it was that I first entered a broadcasting studio and spoke into a microphone. I was eleven years old. I remember the heavy grey drapes on walls and ceiling, the grey corded carpet

1

and the dead, grey sound when one spoke. The microphone was slung on a stand, I remember, that had rubber wheels, and I had to climb on to the conductor's rostrum to reach it when it was my turn to speak. Well, I read my story, and then there were songs to sing and choruses to join in, as we were invited to 'Say It With a Ukulele' — one of the popular songs of the day.

Auntie Cyclone was really Kathleen Garscadden, a professional soprano with a lovely voice, and her songs were among the highlights of Children's Hour for many, many years. But in these early days she was 'Auntie' to everyone, and she and Uncle Mungo (Mungo M. Dewar) and Uncle Alec (A. Swinton Paterson) were tremendous favourites. There were four BBC stations in Scotland in the nineteen-twenties. Glasgow and Aberdeen were what were called 'main stations' and Edinburgh and Dundee were 'relay stations'. A comedian's joke at the time — "I'm taking these rotten eggs to the BBC — to have them re-layed!"

Broadcasting was a wonderful novelty in its early years, but you didn't just turn a switch. You worked at 'listening-in'. You fiddled and messed about with knobs and coils and condensers as you tried to 'tune in'. You heard nothing at first but high-pitched whistling and as you twiddled you caused what was called 'oscillation' — and annoyance to other listeners in the neighbourhood. You fiddled and you twiddled until you eventually got something. You see, people talked in terms of stations they could hear, rather than of programmes. "What foreign stations can you get?" — that was a common question at school. "We can get Munich" — "Huh, that's nothing. My father gets Tokio!" Well, I was blissfully happy just with 5SC, which was the original call-sign for Glasgow. (In Aberdeen it was 2BD).

The timing of programmes was more approximate than accurate. "That's the end of the concert by the Govan Burgh Band", the announcer would say. ("Uncle Mungo to-night" we would whisper knowingly!) "Please stand by for three minutes". We would gratefully 'stand by' for three, four or five minutes, realising perhaps

2

ON MY WAVELENGTH

(those of us who knew what went on!) that while the Govan Burgh Band was being hustled out of the studio, complete with instruments, music and music-stands, the Scottish National Players were being hustled in, with thunder-sheet, wind-machine and other portable sound effects.

As a child, I lived in Ayr, in a house later to disappear, rising from the ashes paradoxically as a fire-station. My brother, John, was the practical one of the family. It was he who made our first wireless-set and fitted it into an oak box. A three-valve set it was, one of the very latest, with all the usual appendages of coils, condensers, dry batteries, rheostats and something called an accumulator, the acid from which, my mother complained, burned holes in her mahogany table! And of course there were wires everywhere. The family must have found it hard to coax me away from the earphones. Of course we had no loudspeaker in those days. Oh no, that was a luxury for us that followed much later. My Lockhart grandmother voiced an opinion that was far from uncommon, when she declared in her characteristically forthright manner, "I wouldn't have one of these confounded loud speakers in my house. Noisy, ugly things. Makes the place sound like a tearoom!"

Most of my early wireless memories are bound up with the Children's Corner, but I do remember how eagerly we listened to The News during the General Strike of 1926. And I remember that once, as a special treat, I was allowed to stay up late — what do you think for? — to hear Big Ben for the first time. And always there were voices. At an early age I became discriminating about voices. At Ayr Academy, one teacher had a great influence over me, for it was she who first infected me with a love of poetry and Shakespeare. You see, with her we didn't just study Shakespeare. We acted the parts. Miss MacPhail was, I now think, a teacher very much in advance of her time. She herself had a lovely speaking voice, with beautiful cadences, and without knowing it, she exemplified the value of good speaking without affectation or artifice. I must tell you that years later, when I went back to Ayr

HOWARD LOCKHART

Academy to judge some speech classes, I was delighted to find Miss MacPhail still there. When I asked her what she remembered about me, she thought for a moment, and then she said softly, "Nothing really. Just that you were a nice, quiet boy!" Ah well! . . .

While I was still at Ayr Academy, I would go on occasional Saturdays and holidays to take part in the Children's Corner in Glasgow. The BBC very soon moved to roomier premises in Blythswood Square. And usually I read a story. Sometimes one I had written myself, or one handed to me by Kathleen just before we went on the air. And of course one sang songs, joined in choruses and took part in the general chit-chat which was completely spontaneous. Eyes were kept firmly on the clock and one learned to judge and extemporise according to circumstances. Years and years later, I used to hear experienced broadcasters marvel at the apparent ease and accuracy with which Kathleen could fill a gap in a programme, with a song or just some impromptu game. But you see, in those early days one learned to be flexible, to deal with any situation as it arose, and above all, to 'keep the heid'!

When not at the studio, I was an avid listener. I joined the Radio Circle. For this we paid ninepence and we were given a badge, with an aerial on it, and, underneath, 5SC Radio Circle written on it. The money went to a fund for providing wireless sets for children's hospitals. And Kathleen ran a spirited Radio Circle Choir with a practice every Saturday morning. And, absurd as it may seem, these rehearsals were actually broadcast! They were presumably used to provide testing material for retailers and dealers at a time when there were no programmes on the air, to demonstrate wireless sets. And then there were a number of highly successful bazaars to raise funds for charity. And two of these I remember vividly. One was held in the City Hall, which was widely used then for concerts and meetings of all kinds. It was rather funny that in the middle 'fifties, the BBC got temporary use of it during alterations to the studio at Queen Margaret Drive, and there, some thirty years after, I found myself once again, announcing orchestral concerts. And it was at that Bazaar, that one of the 'Uncles' — I can't remember which one although I think it was Uncle Mungo — who made a spectacular entrance on a scooter — 1925 style!

Another Bazaar was held in the Church hall at the foot of Woodlands Road. Long before the doors were opened, a queue began to form along the street, and it was soon obvious that the hall simply could not accommodate the crowd that was clamouring to get in. For a short time a rumour began to spread that the floor was going to cave in. And I think this was the first time anybody realised the tremendous power of radio and the popularity of the Aunties and Uncles. They were besieged by autograph hunters, and their photos sold like hot cakes. And proved rather more durable. Oh yes, somewhere to-day, tucked away at the back of a drawer, or in an old faded album, people still come across the autographed photos of Auntie Cyclone, Uncle Mungo and Uncle Alec from those far-off days.

In 1927, I left Ayr Academy and joined my brother, Allan, in Glasgow. He was at the University and I went to the High School. I was fifteen. We stayed with the Lightbodys, Miss Annie and Miss Jessie, in a top-floor flat in Pitt Street. They were wonderful warm-hearted, typically Glasgow people. We stayed with them for years, and they became lifelong friends. Happily for me, the BBC was just around the corner. By this time, Uncle Alec and Uncle Mungo had disappeared into administrative jobs, and various other "uncles" replaced them. Among them, those I particularly remember were Uncle Martyn, Uncle Bob and (not an 'uncle' at all really, but the one who was to have the most influence on my career), 'Longfellow'.

Uncle Martyn, that was Martyn C. Webster, was an excellent announcer, and he also produced one of radio's first concert parties, "The Radioptimists", big favourites in their day.

5

Martyn had an impish sense of mischief. Once at the microphone, he floored me with the remark, "Rather bold of you, wasn't it Howard, to come up to the studio dressed in only a bathing-suit?" In my tall, gangling teens, he always used to address me as "little Howard Lockhart!" In due course, he went south to Birmingham and then to London, as one of radio's most successful drama producers.

Uncle Bob was Rex Kingsley. He had been an announcer both in Glasgow and Dundee, and he was also an excellent actor. Later he specialised in sports commentaries, and I can remember sitting by his side in the commentator's box at Ibrox and Hampden, and marvelling at the adroit manner in which he described the game so accurately and so graphically. In the fly-leaf of my copy of his book, 'I Saw Stars' he has written this. "To my dear friend, Howard, whose courtesy and complete imperturbability during BBC rehearsals often made temperamental artists like the author feel very humble. R. E. Kingsley". I must say I'm rather proud of that inscription.

Longfellow was Andrew Stewart, named by Kathleen because of his height, and he was one of the most popular of all Children's Hour personalities. He was a fine reader of stories. He always used to begin them, I remember, with "Once upon a time, for all the best stories begin that way — at least mine always do . . ." I think his most popular one was "The Gingerbread Man" — "Run, run, as fast as you can, you can't catch me, I'm the Gingerbread Man!" He was also a popular singer, specialising in 'The Lum Hat Wantin' the Croon'. He'd say, "The key of doh, please Barbara, and not too high!"

Barbara Laing was for many years pianist in the Children's Hour and she and Andrew Bryson shared duties as official accompanists. They were wonderful players, come to that they were wonderful people. And one other uncle I must mention was the philatelist, A. K. MacDonald, and naturally we called him Uncle

Phil, because his talks to stamp collectors were so popular for many years.

During my Glasgow High School years, I got my first intoxicating taste of stage acting, in the well-organised dramatic club. Here, in the person of Mr. A. Parry Gunn, was someone who was to have a lasting effect on my subsequent career, although of course I was quite unaware of it at the time. Parry Gunn, a man of wide cultural and theatrical experience, with a beautifully modulated voice and polished charm, came to school once a week to take us for Shakespeare and drama. How lucky we were. He produced the plays we did at the end of the Christmas and summer terms. To Parry Gunn I shall always be indebted for what he taught me and for what I learned, merely by watching him at work. A long time afterwards, when I was doing my own stage productions, I often used to find myself using methods I'd seen Parry Gunn use, or indulging in a trick I had unconsciously absorbed from him. My very first part consisted of four lines as a messenger in the Beaumont & Fletcher Elizabethan play, 'The Knight of the Burning Pestle'. But as time went on, I got bigger parts and these stage appearances were for me the highlights of my school career.

Kathleen came to see our plays, she was awfully good that way. And so did a tall, handsome, blonde lady, escorted by one of the teachers. We learned with awe that this was Nan Scott of the Scottish National Players. Her appearance and presence couldn't have been more impressive if she'd been royalty itself — which, in a way, she was!

Often after school I'd rush to a call-box and phone to Kathleen. "May I come up to Children's Hour?" I'd say, and I don't remember ever getting a rebuff, far less a refusal, and off I'd go, just to sit in the studio and watch. Sometimes I'd get a few lines or crowd work in a play, or help with the sound effects. I remember thinking I'd really got somewhere when I was allowed to open and shut the effects door in a play that had such eminent players in it as Moultrie Kelsall and Elsie Brotchie.

They were among the big names in radio drama in those days. Others included Elliot Mason, Jean Taylor Smith, Nell Ballantyne, Meg Buchanan, Nan Scott, Grace McChlery, Catherine Fletcher, Bertha Waddell, who was to become famous later for her Children's Theatre, R. B. Wharrie, Hal D. Stewart, Halbert Tatlock, who specialised in giants and sinister parts, James Urquhart, Ian Sadler, Harold Wightman, James Gibson and Charles R. M. Brookes.

Elliot Mason was the outstanding name among Scottish players at that time. Eventually she went to London where she became a much sought-after character actress. She also established a kind of home from home for Scottish players in London. She was a large, matronly lady, very bright and cheerful. In 1938, when I was with the BBC in London for the first time, she put herself out to show me hospitality and to introduce me to interesting people in the theatre. I know that I am by no means the only beginner she encouraged and, like so many others, I have cause to remember Elliot Mason with affection and gratitude.

I can't remember when I received my first BBC fee, but all my earliest experience was gratuitous. Frankly, it never occurred to me that I ought to be paid. I was too thrilled and delighted to be permitted to be in the studio; I thought then how lucky I was. I still think I was lucky. However one day I was offered a contract to take part in a Children's Hour play, and what do you think it was for? Ten and sixpence! And ten and sixpence my fee remained for many years to come. Did I think the amount was modest? I did not! I would gladly have paid, just for the privilege of being what I regarded as a real professional.

Mostly, like all radio actors, I played a variety of parts in each play. I was never much good at disguising my voice though. I used to envy the versatility of people like Ian Sadler and Rex Kingsley. I played Laurie, the boy friend in 'Little Women' and

David Balfour in Stevenson's 'Kidnapped'. I was also Prince Charming in 'Cinderella'. Yes, one Saturday afternoon I was in my digs in Pitt Street, when Miss Jessie told me there was some-one at the door from the BBC. And this was to say that somebody in the cast had failed to appear and I was wanted to deputise. I tore up there to find that not only was I to play Prince Charming, but I had songs to learn. Well, somehow I got through it, and once again had cause to be grateful for the fortuitous hand that had guided me to digs just a stone's throw from the BBC.

I remember my delight at being cast in the leading part in a schoolboy adventure play. It was a serial too, a cliffhanger. At one stage I was left in some diabolical situation at the end of an episode, and eagerly awaited the arrival of the next script to learn how I escaped. Alas! I never did find out. No more contracts arrived. So on my next visit to the BBC, I asked what had happened. "Oh well", came the reply, "it was all a bit impossible, so we decided just to drop it!" So I never knew what happened to me . . .

And then came Toytown and Larry the Lamb and this was definitely a landmark for me. The scripts for Toytown were originally supplied locally to each Region and done with a local cast. But later, London took over with Derek McCulloch as Larry, which of course he had been playing in the London Region. It was just pure luck that I got the part in Scotland. Originally it had been played by Bettine Luke in a number of episodes in which I had played tiny parts. Well, one day, in the manner of romantic fiction, Bettine was unable to take part, and at the last minute the part was given to me. And from then on, I was Larry the Lamb for a number of years.

When I was twenty-one, my broadcasting fee was raised to one guinea. Oh yes, it had remained until then at ten and sixpence. And even when I had to travel up from Ayr, during the long University holidays, it never occurred to me to ask for travelling expenses. I was much too scared that the BBC would find out I

9

was not living in Glasgow and drop me in favour of somebody who was. You see, I didn't have much confidence in my work. I never have been blessed with much self-confidence.

There was one person I secretly envied at the time and that was Elsie Payne. Elsie was about my own age and she specialised in little boy parts. In these she was absolutely superb. Even to-day, nobody has surpassed her. Whenever a producer needed someone to be a small boy, Elsie was the obvious choice. Everybody loved Elsie Payne and her death in 1953 robbed radio of one of its finest and most sensitive performers. But, as I say, twenty years earlier I envied her. I'd say to her, "Gosh, Elsie, how lucky you are to get into all these evening plays". You see, I longed to get into something more adult, more sophisticated than Children's Hour. I even began, let's face it, to be feeling a bit ashamed of my long association with what was derisively dismissed at school as 'kid's stuff'! Kathleen Garscadden relates that initially I used to end my letters to her "your affectionate nephew, Howard". Then suddenly I cooled into "your respectful listener". But this exactly reflected my attitude at the time.

And then to my great joy and surprise I did get an evening broadcast. Andrew Stewart booked me to do crowd work and sound effects in a programme called,' 'Knockendoch Hauds Hallowe'en'. Mrs. Helen Mitchell had created a fictional farm called Knockendoch based on recollections of her own childhood in Dumfriesshire. The Knockendoch series had been very successful in Children's Hour and this particular edition was designed on a more ambitious scale to attract an adult, evening audience. And it apparently proved equally successful and was the first of many. I took it for granted that I'd be in the next one too. But I wasn't! I wasn't even asked. It was a big blow to my ego and no doubt did me a lot of good. For one thing, it taught me never to take things for granted. And, above all, to wait until contracts are signed before any kind of self-congratulation.

ON MY WAVELENGTH

In 1930, I left school and went to Glasgow University, graduating M.A. three years later. On the whole I enjoyed the life, especially as it enabled me to go on broadcasting and acting. I became increasingly interested in the spoken word and had lessons from Parry Gunn. He gave me a number of character studies to learn by heart and he directed me and coached me in their performance. In this way I acquired a repertoire of varied items and was soon accepting public engagements as an 'elocutionist'! And in the next few years I appeared in town halls, Church halls, school halls, anywhere and everywhere, without any kind of reward, beyond a cup of tea and a vote of thanks. I did comic readings, I even did tragic readings. And when I say readings, that is precisely what they were not. They were memorised until I was word-perfect. And there was no prompter to help. I must have been outrageous! I shudder to recall that I even had the brass neck to perpetrate my interpretation of the 'dagger' speech from 'Macbeth' on an unsuspecting audience. Can you credit it? It must have been dire! But the point was that I was getting experience. From Parry Gunn, I learned how to talk and how to walk. He taught me how to make an entrance, how to talk on a public platform, how to walk on to a public platform, how to move and how to project the voice. The audiences taught me the rest — how to time a laugh, and, conversely, how to kill one. How to work up to a climax. The precise moment when to break it. How long to hold a pause. Mind you, I'm not suggesting I was successful at doing any of these things, but the point was that I tried to be. And I recognised and admired artists who were.

One of these was Willie McCulloch. He was a very popular and highly experienced entertainer. He did character studies that were lifelike in their reflection of recognisable types, and he was a master of timing and technique. He knew just how to play with an audience as if it were a sensitive and responsive instrument. When I later came to know and work with the great Will Fyffe, I immediately recognised the same uncanny ability. Both of them

11

could have an audience laughing helplessly one minute, and, in an instant, create an atmosphere of dead silence, with the audience almost transfixed in pathos. And I watched and I watched, always analysing, always trying to learn more. I was fascinated by the art of the performer.

Almost on leaving school, I began to get engagements all round Glasgow, Ayr and the west of Scotland. Modest ones, it's true, and almost always unpaid, but providing me with what I wanted most — experience. And I loved every minute of it. Through Parry Gunn, I got an introduction to one of Glasgow's oldest and most successful amateur dramatic companies — the Players' Club. Their system was to have a repertory of about half a dozen one-act plays at the beginning of each season, and to tour these round the hospitals and institutions in Glasgow and the neighbourhood. This again provided me with invaluable experience. Staging and furniture varied from place to place and sometimes we would have to change our dialogue as we went along. All this taught us to be adaptable and inventive. It also placed great emphasis both on self-reliance and on team-work. In my second season with the Players I was allowed to produce as well as act.

My father frequently used to question me doubtfully about the amount of time I was 'frittering away' — "neglecting the substance for the shadow", as he put it! And if I tentatively suggested I preferred the shadow, I was told in no uncertain terms that one needed something more substantial to live on. Let there be no mistake, he had my welfare very much to heart. And his advice was that I settle into a steady career first, and then sit back and enjoy my acting as a hobby. And so it was decided that I should follow my brother, Allan, in studying for law.

Meanwhile, I was making headway BBC-wise. To my great surprise and delight, I was asked to take over the presentation of Children's Hour one summer when Kathleen was on holiday. Now for me this was all a tremendous thrill and I revelled in the responsibility and excitement of it all. Mind you, she had left vast and detailed preparation, so there wasn't very much left to chance, and I couldn't really go very far wrong. I also found myself in a number of plays, most of which were produced by either Andrew Stewart or Gordon Gildard, both of whom taught me a great deal. Andrew Stewart, in particular, encouraged me to get experience, and for him I did my first solo act in a Variety show. Yes, I did a Para Handy sketch by Neil Munro, and a Hollywood skit that I had written myself. It was also from Andrew that I got my first tentative experience in radio production. This was in a hospital sketch, in which the principal parts were played by Elsie Payne and a very talented and versatile actress called Elvira Airlie. It had lots of hospital gags in it, of course, and a small part for me as one of the patients. Andrew entrusted some of the rehearsals to me. Of course I loved every absorbing minute of it. I can date my interest in radio production from that simple hospital sketch.

Andrew Stewart was a perfectionist, relentless sometimes until he got just the effect he wanted. I remember once at a Toytown rehearsal when I was being — oh I don't know, indifferent, I wasn't concentrating. "Howard", he said, "Howard, just because you're a lamb, there's no need to sound so woolly"! I knew the moment he said it exactly what he meant. One day he asked me if I'd like to help him out, by doing some announcing for him in the evenings. Would I indeed? "You can bring your books with you", he said, "and study between programmes". Well I can't say I was able to do much studying of the kind Andrew doubtless had in mind, but I was able to gain invaluable experience of announcing, even if most of the programmes seemed to be Brass Band Concerts and topical talks. Andrew himself coached me and criticised me constantly and severely. Microphones were less sensitive and flexible than they are to-day, and one was taught above all to speak clearly. Andrew kept emphasising that many of our listeners, in fact perhaps most of them, especially in the country places, were up in years, perhaps a bit slow in the uptake and it was imperative therefore to speak slowly and with care. To-day, with the advance of technical development, the microphone is much more responsive in reproduction, which is all to the good. But the quality of speech has, in my view, deteriorated in the process. Diction to-day is often indifferent and sometimes downright slovenly, not to say scruffy!

My recollection of these early announcing days brings back the names of many fine singers who were much in demand. The sopranos included Mary Ferrier, Ella Gardner, Amy Samuel, Janette Sclanders, and the contraltos — Crue Davidson, Anne Ballantyne, Jenny Black, Flora Blythman (what a lovely voice Flora Blythman had), and Agnes Duncan, famous later with the Scottish Junior Singers. And among the males, Elliot Dobie, Alexander MacGregor, Ian MacPherson, Robert Watson, Matthew Nisbet and Matthew Dickie, and, of course, Alexander Carmichael. And this was the time when the popularity of Scottish Dance Music was undergoing a great revival and I particularly remember announcing Margaret Smart and her Reel Players, the John McArthur Quintet, Lena Blackman and the Heather Sextet and many others.

I loved announcing and everything connected with programmes, except the 'balancing' of the microphone in relation to the broadcaster. The placing of the mike is a highly skilled technical operation, now done by skilled technicians, trained for the job. But we had to do it ourselves and it was very much a hit or a miss. In the early days it was quite common for the announcer to say, "Will you just stand by, while I move the mike a little nearer the piano?" This would be followed by a noise like the rumble of thunder, while the mike on its stand was trundled over the carpet.

In announcing, I often had to play records to fill gaps between programmes. Recitals by Christopher Stone in London were becoming enormously popular and I managed to get Andrew Stewart to allow me to arrange a selection of Scottish records under the title, 'Scotch Broth'. Well, this apparently proved an acceptable dish because it continued for many years, and I think I can say that I thus became, through 'Scotch Broth', Scotland's very first disc-jockey, although such an expression belonged very much to the future!

CHAPTER 2

THE GOLDEN YEARS

ALTHOUGH my heart was very much in broadcasting, I saw no prospect of a career in it. After graduating M.A., in 1933, I became a law apprentice in a Glasgow office, taking classes at the same time for a law degree. The whole idea filled me with dismay. Not because I had any real prejudice against becoming a lawyer, but simply because I dreaded the curtailment of my BBC work. I discussed this with Andrew Stewart and he suggested that, once I had my degree, I might be able to get a post as legal adviser to the BBC. But this was not at all what I had in mind! I viewed the immediate future with misgivings. Once I had started working in a law office, how could I expect to continue my BBC work, particularly Children's Hour and Toytown? It was precisely here that events took a decisive turn in my favour. You see, when I presented myself before the senior partner of the legal firm I was to join, he said to me in the course of our interview, "I hear you sometimes speak on the wireless. Do you know Aunt Kathleen?" Did I know her? At my answer his face crinkled into a wide smile, and he said, "She's a very nice lady, isn't she? She's a client of ours, you know". Well, my mind skipped ahead. It was highly unlikely that, in the event of her needing my help, it would be withheld. And this was precisely how it turned out. There was still Toytown and Larry the Lamb, and not infrequent phone calls from Kathleen or her secretary in the mornings, asking me to report to Blythswood Square later in the day. I'd get permission from the senior partner, and off I'd trot to the BBC.

But, as one door opened, another closed. They wanted an announcer in Edinburgh, and I thought I'd get the job, as I'd been doing announcing. But I didn't! It went to Douglas Moodie, a young actor, much in demand to play romantic roles in radio plays. And he later became a highly successful producer. Well, after this blow, I began to revive when I heard that Andrew Stewart was to have a permanent assistant in Glasgow. Well, I could hardly miss, this time. I could! The job went to James Fergusson (now Sir James Fergusson of Kilkerran, Bt.) who had academic qualifications much more impressive than mine.

Well, now that Andrew had an assistant, there was no more announcing for me, but I continued in Children's Hour and from time to time in evening plays. Most of the leading players in Scottish radio plays were from the Scottish National Players, and eventually I was lucky enough to get a part in one of their stage productions. They represented the very peak in Scottish dramatic achievement. I was not immediately accepted. First, I was auditioned by W. G. Fay, the Irish producer, who was their director for a time. But it turned out they were looking for a small boy, and I was much too tall, said Mr. Fay. Apparently I was supposed to sit on the leading lady's knee! I had also tried unsuccessfully to get a part with the Brandon Thomas Players. They were a very popular company at the Glasgow Theatre Royal. However, I was ultimately cast as the Pedant for the SNP (when those initials stood only for Scottish National Players and had no political significance!). This was in a large-scale production of 'The Taming of the Shrew' at the Lyric Theatre. The producer was Wilfrid Fletcher, who was brought up specially from London. For me it was an experience of unalloyed joy. The cast was a very happy one and included players both established and to become well-known. Nan Scott was the Shrew, Graham Squire played Petruchio, Marjorie Dalziel was Bianca. And in other parts, James Gibson, Hal D. Stewart, Tom Smith, Ernest Mace and Archie Henry, who was to become a highly popular BBC announcer later on. Nan Scott was superb, in a production of great elegance, and my happiness reached its zenith one night when Nan grasped my arm as I came off-stage, and said in her rather grand, expansive

17

manner, "Excellent bit of character work, Howard!" That was for me perhaps the ultimate accolade!

And so there I was, enjoying myself very much, both in the theatre and in the studio. And there were frequent parties, given by Andrew Stewart or Kathleen Garscadden, when six or eight of us would go to the Plaza or the Albert Ballroom. Others in those parties included Barbara Laing, Elsie Payne, Bettine Luke, Sydney MacEwan, who was a student and already becoming well-known for his beautiful tenor voice. And there was a young journalist and script-writer called Jack House who also joined us from time to time. Sometimes Kathleen took me along with her to join in duets at concerts. We used to sing 'The Crookit Bawbee' and songs of that kind. Kathleen was always greatly in demand.

Spending as much time as I did in enjoying the activities that came so much more easily to me, and gave me such a feeling of satisfaction, it's hardly surprising that I was making precious little headway with my legal studies. I did just manage to scrape through the exams, but the significance lay in the fact that I shouldn't have cared much if I hadn't! All the same, I liked the office and it taught me a great deal for which I've since been grateful. I got on well with the staff who were sympathetic and friendly. All except one apprentice who, reasonably enough, resented the time I was allowed off for broadcasting. For my part, I tholed the office work. I did what I was told and sometimes tried out my acting experiments on the staff. One day as I was practising my George Arliss expression in the mirror, the senior partner, unseen by me, emerged from his office, saying quietly as he passed me, "Toothache, Lockhart?" Sometimes I used to exaggerate and dramatise my depression, once striking an attitude and declaring histrionically to the friendly secretaries, that I was "drinking the dregs of despair"! Well, they hooted with laughter at my melodramatic excess and, before I knew it, an office catch-phrase was born, and I was continually being assailed with,

ON MY WAVELENGTH

"Drinking the dregs again, Howard?" When I came to leave the office, one of the entries in an autograph-book they compiled read, "No more dregs for Howard!"

Well, life continued thus for about two years. At the back of my mind, I felt that, sooner or later, I would be faced with some colossally dramatic situation which would resolve matters for me. But it didn't turn out like that at all. Except insofar as suddenly, and quite unexpectedly, a decision was forced on me. One afternoon, the junior partner sent for me and handed me a document to deliver in the city, with instructions to wait and bring it back. Well, I told him that the senior partner had already given me permission to get off early for a broadcast that day. He looked at me with an expression of undisguised fury, all the more frightening, because normally he was the most amiable of men, and banging his fist on the desk, he said, "You're here to do as you're told! Not to spend our time at the BBC. Now, go and obey my orders!" I can remember how, as I pulled the door behind me — I remember the handle was low and I had to bend down to reach it — I realised in that instant that now, here, at last it had arrived — the moment of decision. I knew precisely what I was going to do. Oh there was no doubt of that. I went to the BBC and did the broadcast.

But that night I made up my mind. The pretence of becoming a lawyer must end. I would give it up. I'd probably be sacked in the morning anyway. I deserved to be, for disobeying an order. All the same, I confess it, now that it had arrived, I faced what was coming with apprehension. First thing next morning, I went directly to carry out the orders as instructed. Then I went back to the office. My heart was in my boots, fluttering there, as I pushed open the swing doors and entered. I took off my coat and bowler hat and hung them up in the cloakroom with my umbrella. Then I picked up the document and knocked on the junior partner's door. He was out, as it happened, so I left the document on his desk. And the rest of the morning passed in an agony of

suspense. I heard him coming in. I waited. And waited. And —
nothing! Nothing. Just an anti-climax. Whether he just hadn't
noticed or just hadn't bothered, I never found out, but nothing
ever happened. Except that I had made up my mind.

That week-end I talked things over with my father. As always,
he was sympathetic, although his disappointment was evident.
"What are you going to do then?" was the obvious question. Well,
I decided to concentrate on getting all the experience I could in
broadcasting, in entertaining, until such time as I could get a job
with the BBC. It seems extraordinary to me now, but in spite of
the disappointment and the set-backs I apparently never doubted
that I would! And, sure enough, that's how things worked out.
Within a few months, there was a vacancy for an announcer in
Edinburgh, then the BBC headquarters in Scotland. And off I went
to London for an interview. Now you'd think, wouldn't you, that
such a momentous milestone in my life would have been etched
in my memory indelibly? But no, not at all. I don't remember
anything about that interview. I was hopeless at interviews anyway,
being always so insistent on pointing out the things I couldn't
do, rather than boasting about those I could!

Anyway, I got the job — at £260 per annum! Five quid a week!
I remember being asked if I thought this reasonable. Well, weigh-
ing it against the few bob I earned as a law apprentice, not to
mention the joyful prospect of being in the BBC, I exercised
restraint and said I thought it was. And so, in 1935, there I was
— a fulltime BBC Announcer. I was elated at the idea of going
to headquarters in Edinburgh, and all the glorious opportunities
that lay ahead. But I had misgivings too. Only vague ones. But
enough to make me say to a colleague in Glasgow, "You know
my one ambition is to come back here, permanently, some day".
I did too. But hardly foreseeing that before then, the world would
be turned upside down in a second World War.

Joining the BBC staff in the year 1935 meant that I was arriving
at the peak, the very peak of the Reith period. Now these have

ON MY WAVELENGTH

been called the golden years of broadcasting. I'd certainly say they were the golden years of Scottish broadcasting. Since then there have been tremendous technical advances of course, especially in the development of tape recording, but there was — a quality, an identity about broadcasting in Scotland, during the few years prior to the outbreak of war, that has, in my view, never really been equalled.

This was the time when the BBC Scottish Orchestra came into being in Edinburgh, with J. Mouland Begbie as leader and Guy Warrack as its first conductor. One of the curious features of the Edinburgh studio was that the announcements had to be made from a cubicle on the floor above, and this often led to complications, making liaison between the announcers and the conductor difficult, to say the least of it. A flight of steep stone, grey-carpeted stairs had to be negotiated, often at speed, and there was one step out of alignment with the rest, I never could remember which one. And how we announcers cursed that irregular step!

The concerts by the BBC Scottish were a treat musically, but frankly I was unsure of myself with both Ian Whyte, who was head of the music department, and Guy Warrack, and the difficulty of keeping in touch with them during broadcasts always used to worry me, not to mention that damned stair! Continuity between programmes to-day is maintained by the Continuity Announcer, as he's called, in a Continuity Suite, and he has telephones and turntables, records and tapes and every possible facility. The nearest we had to that was a tiny, airless studio, only a cubicle really, with room for one chair, one desk and one announcer! The microphone hung suspended over the desk and our only other means of communication to the Control Room was from a telephone, outside the door, believe it or not! From the cubicle we announced, we read news bulletins, weather forecasts and, it seemed to me, interminable lists of market prices for farmers. We spent hours in the claustrophobic atmosphere of that

21

stuffy little room, staring at a wall disconcertingly dark and 'busy' in pattern.

A large amount of our announcing time was taken up with broadcasts to schools. And I longed to see what happened at the receiving end, and so it was arranged for me to visit a school in Portobello. Well, I was dismayed. The children were interested enough, but the teacher was not! She even managed to mis-spell on the blackboard one of the subject-headings that had been spelled out slowly and correctly by the broadcaster. One of my favourites in schools programmes was Herbert Wiseman. He was a superb broadcaster with an appealing voice and an irresistible manner. "Good afternoon, boys and girls," he'd say. And he'd wait for their silent response before proceeding. At the school there was a roar, of "Good afternoon, sir!" from every voice in that hall. And it seemed to me that this was a perfect example of broadcasting technique, where the broadcaster and the listener come together in one combined act. I am not ashamed to admit that I have copied this technique in my greetings programme, when I say, "How are you to-day?" and I wait for the answer in my mind's ear.

In the evenings, between programmes, we announcers used to spend a good deal of time in the Control Room on the top floor at Queen Street, where there is a lovely view of Granton and the Forth. And I got quite chummy with the engineers and often used to make the tea, when they were busy and I was not. They were a very cheery, friendly bunch. Once, however, I'm afraid I did put my foot in it! You see, if there was a break in transmission, a 'technical hitch', as it was called, the announcer, had to broadcast an apology, as soon as the fault had been rectified. Well, on this occasion, I made the apology all right, adding that it was "due to circumstances outwith our control". Well they thought, or pretended to think, I had said, "UP with our Control!" And I never heard the end of it.

Of course, like most announcers, I did make mistakes from time to time. I once said "Si Mes Vers Avaient Des Ailes" was by Mendelssohn, when it's by Reynaldo Hahn. I was confusing 'If My Songs Were Only Winged' with 'On Wings of Song'. And once when I gave a list of book titles at the end of a book review, I called one of them 'King James the Sixth and I, using the first personal pronoun after the manner of 'The King and I'. I was blissfully unaware of my lapse until the programme was over, and a hysterical lady studio-manager reminded me that King James the Sixth of Scotland was King James the First of England! Was my Scottish face red? Another time, I gravely offended band-leader Harry Roy by admitting to him that I did not know he required two pianos in the studio for his band. He looked at me with an expression of withering scorn, **"Everybody** knows that Harry Roy has two pianos!" he said in tones of ice. True enough, everyone except me apparently did. And I should have remembered the Tiger-Ragamuffins, Ivor Moreton and Dave Kaye.

When VIP'S were expected in the evenings, we were expected to don dinner-jackets and for this we got a small annual dress-allowance. I have heard it said that announcers wore evening-dress just to read the news bulletin. Not true at all. Formal dress was worn purely out of deference to anyone who might arrive at the studios in evening-dress. Smoking in the studios was absolutely forbidden, VIP's notwithstanding. And there were no exceptions to this rule. And quite rightly I think. Nowadays it's quite common to find a studio thick with fug and the smell of stale smoke.

Although I had never seen Lord Reith, his authority was very very much in evidence. In later years this has come to be regarded as something rather tyrannical and inhibiting. I never found it so. I rather like the following quotation from the dedication of London's Broadcasting House:—'That good seed may bring forth a good harvest. That all things hostile to peace and purity may be banished from this house. And that the people inclining

23

their ear to whatever things are beautiful and honest and of good report, may tread the path of wisdom and uprightness'. I like that. I don't say we came anywhere near achieving this goal, but at least we had a star for our wagon, however frail and rickety the latter might be.

About this time, my parents were crossing the Atlantic on an ocean liner when they learned that Lord Reith was on board. My father would have liked to speak to him, but he didn't see any obvious way of bringing this about. However, by judiciously observing his habit of perambulating round the deck each day at a fixed time, my father contrived to be in his path and introduced himself by mentioning that I had recently joined the BBC, as a very junior member of staff. His Lordship muttered something non-committal and after a word or two, they parted. A few days later, a note was handed to my father, which read, "I have been in touch with my office and I made enquiries about your son. I think you will be pleased to know that he is shaping well in our organisation". It was signed by Lord Reith.

In Edinburgh, the most enjoyable part of my work, and the least expected, turned out once again to be Children's Hour. It was run by Cecile Walton, who was known as Wendy. This was very different from working in Kathleen's programmes. Oh no, there were no conundrums here, no inconsequential ad libbing. It wasn't exactly impersonal but certainly much more formal. Cold and unfriendly, said our critics. But Wendy's programmes were packed with material, mostly historical or legendary, and nothing was left to chance. Cecile Walton was a lady of wide cultural perception and sympathetic understanding. She was an idealist, a dreamer. "Wendy's rather vague", people would say. This was quite inaccurate. Abstracted sometimes, yes, but not vague.

Gradually she took over the role of producer, leaving the actual presentation of programmes in subordinate hands. I helped in this capacity. So did Enid Maxwell (Tinkerbell) and, later, Betty Ogilvie and Gladys Sutherland. Other popular personalities

24

included 'Heather Jock' (Andrew P. Wilson) and Uncle Dudley (Dudley Stuart White) with his fine, baritone voice. We also had regular visits from Uncle Tom (Tom Gillespie) of the Edinburgh Zoo to report in his genial, kindly manner the latest zoo news. Sometimes he would bring Bobo with him. Bobo was a very large ape and he was a great favourite with the children. He wasn't such a favourite with one of the secretaries — after he'd bitten her! Once, when she was planning a public broadcast from the Edinburgh studio, Wendy remarked, with a perfectly straight face, "Of course my biggest attractions are Bobo and Auntie Kathleen!"

As time went on, Wendy was giving me more and more to do in Children's Hour. I adapted and read a number of books for children, and, looking back on this period of my life, I find my impressions are dominated by memories of Children's Hour, Wendy and her vivacious secretary, Binnie Crawford ('Puppy'). When Wendy eventually left the BBC, her place was taken as Children's Hour Organiser by Christine Orr, one of the best-loved and most delightful people ever to be on the BBC staff. I greatly enjoyed my work in Children's Hour, and I quite enjoyed being an announcer, but I wasn't altogether happy, and I wasn't sorry when I heard a rumour that a change was coming my way.

Moultrie Kelsall had been running the Aberdeen station, practically single-handed, for several years, and doing so with conspicuous success. But it was proving impossible for one man to run an office, look after staff administration, and do all the programme work as well. Hugh MacPhee, brother of my old friend, James MacPhee, the Gaelic singer from the Blythswood Square days, had been in Aberdeen to cover Gaelic programmes, but he was returning to Glasgow, and the idea was that I should go to Aberdeen as Moultrie's assistant.

Moultrie Kelsall had a reputation as a brilliant, if mercurial producer, and I should certainly learn a lot from him. But I was doubtful of my own ability to reflect his particular talents. I discussed my prospects with Wendy, knowing I would get from her

25

an honest appraisal of the situation. She was unequivocal. This would be a wonderful opportunity for me to learn the whole business of broadcasting, producing, announcing, planning and the entire administrative process. "Not only that", she added with a smile, "you'll be taking over Children's Hour and making it your own!" So it seemed the experience could hardly fail to be good for me.

And so it came about. On a cold, grey day in April, 1936, my mind a mixture of anticipation and mild foreboding, I took the train north from Edinburgh to Aberdeen.

CHAPTER 3

ABERDEEN ANIMALS

I 'VE said it before and I'll say it again. Aberdeen, even after two world trips and many faraway places, remains my favourite city. And yet, for me, first impressions were hardly favourable. It was a rotten day, for one thing. Cold and dreary, when Hugh MacPhee met me at the Joint Station. Passing the Tivoli on our right, he led me up an interminable flight of stone steps emerging on Union Street, wet and windy, bustling with people, noisy with trams. Crossing, we made our way down a narrow, paved street, until we reached 15 Belmont Street, the Aberdeen BBC.

Before leaving Edinburgh, I had been told, "You're being sent to help Moultrie Kelsall. Do everything he tells you, even if it means going out to his home at Cults and pushing the pram!" He was married to pianist Ruby Duncan, and they had an infant son. Once, weeks later, when Moultrie was out of town, Ruby arrived at Belmont Street, panting from exertions of shopping while carrying the baby. Would I be a dear and give her a hand to the bus stop? She would take the parcels if I would take the baby. People were smiling as we passed them on our way up Belmont Street to the Wallace Statue, me with the baby on my shoulder, Ruby laden with parcels. "A very young father, people will be saying!" smiled Ruby. She had a delightfully soft, musical voice, and a manner that some people described as 'rather vague'.

Once Moultrie asked me to join Ruby, Leo Hunter, the BBC Outside Broadcasts man, and himself on a visit to the Tivoli to see Dave Willis, whom we all much admired. It was a pleasant, mild evening as we walked down Bridge Street. Ruby, I remember, was wearing a long, black dress, and complaining of the heat. In the theatre she mentioned the general stuffiness. After a visit to the ladies' room at the interval, she returned to her seat with a

27

B

smile on her lips. "Don't tell Moultrie", she whispered to me, "I changed in such a hurry before we came out, I've still got my skirt on under my dress!"

Working for Moultrie Kelsall was certainly never dull. It was, on the contrary, inspiring, exciting, exhilarating, exhausting, irritating and sometimes downright infuriating. Dynamic is the word for Moultrie. Always on the go. One thing I particularly liked about him. He didn't have moods. But, like most people with abundant energy and drive, he had little patience with those unable to keep up with him.

He had a tremendous capacity for work, and if I often felt unable to maintain the pressure at which he worked, I never failed to appreciate the opportunities he provided for learning about radio production. Outside the BBC I was constantly hearing him criticised for employing in all his programmes, the same coterie of artists, 'the same old clique' people would say! All producers face the same charge, for all producers like to work with people they know and whose experience they can rely on. And experience was essential in a Kelsall show, where anything might happen.

Remember that, in those days, there were no recorded programmes, every broadcast being actually performed as it went on the air. With Moultrie, changes in the script during transmission were quite common. A hand, a pencil, would appear over one's shoulder, while one was standing at the mike, and a cut would be indicated with an arrow and some scores. Occasionally, new pages of script were being typed for the end of the show, while the beginning was actually on the air, and these would be handed, one at a time, to the performers at the microphone.

He therefore depended on experienced artists, quick on the uptake, and not easily flustered. Further, the very nature of the relationship between a producer and his cast makes it imperative for him to work in harmony with them, and therefore to have people around him whom he likes. One disagreeable person —

sometimes called a 'nark' — can wreck the state of mutual confidence and respect, and ruin a show. Therefore we tend to employ those we like, those who become our friends — 'the same old clique', if you like. Moultrie Kelsall was no different from others in this respect. With Aberdeen being a smaller community, it was more noticeable, that's all.

It was in Aberdeen, under Moultrie Kelsall, that I got such valuable training. For one thing, he showed he was willing to take chances by trusting me with production, right from the start. The very day I arrived, he indicated a large pile of scripts, along with bundles of files relative to Children's Hour programmes, and said tersely, "Here, these are yours!" And so my first assignment turned out to be the Aberdeen Animals.

It never ceases to surprise me that, although the Aberdeen Animals existed for only a few years before their demise on the outbreak of war in 1939, they are still missed, even to-day. Their impact, for a once-weekly broadcast, was quite extraordinary, and they rank among the most popular fictional characters in Scottish radio.

As elsewhere in the early days of wireless, the Aberdeen Children's Hour had been a general get-together in each day's broadcasting, under such well-loved personalities as R. E. Jeffrey, Christine Crowe (Auntie Chris) and Winifred Manners (Auntie Win). When Moultrie Kelsall took over, he invented a group of animals, with himself as Brer Rabbit, Addie Ross as Miss Mouse and Ruby Duncan as Squirrel. Their human friends included Granny Mutch (Christine Crowe) and, later and logically, Grandfather More (Arthur Black). The Animals represented the children's point of view, with Brer Rabbit as the mischievous ringleader, Miss Mouse the capable if rather prim, older sister and Squirrel, the baby. Moultrie ingeniously adapted in terms of sound, the successful technique of popular comics of the day, like 'Puck' and 'Rainbow', where animals with human attributes were the central figures.

HOWARD LOCKHART

Taking over these programmes, which Moultrie had brought to such a peak of popularity was no sinecure. "Will it be Howard the Horse?" he asked. "Could we make it Howard the Hare?" I volunteered. We did. And there was the inevitable Press comment about the strange metamorphosis from lamb to hare!

For the next four years, the Aberdeen Animals were mine. People loved them. Wrote to them. Sent them presents. At Christmas, when we appealed for toys for hospitals, we could hardly move along corridors crammed with parcels and boxes, overflowing from offices and studios already packed to capacity.

Moultrie, as Brer Rabbit, became a less frequent contributor to programmes, after he handed over to me, but his songs were always in great demand, and especially his quickfire rendering of 'The Wee Cooper of Fife'. Addie Ross and Ruby Duncan were my constant companions in the programme. Addie Ross was a most versatile and accomplished broadcaster, both in singing and acting. Her strong, slightly edgy speaking voice made a perfect contrast with the soft, rather baby tones of Ruby Duncan as Squirrel. Ruby excelled in piano syncopation, but was a brilliant all-round pianist, with an uncanny ability to improvise and transpose at sight. We lost Squirrel in due course, when she and Moultrie went to London, and we replaced her with Nan Davidson, who made a genial successor. We called her Glow Worm, because she 'shone in silence' as a non-speaking character. Others who came and went in our Animal Kingdom included Geeraw Giraffe (Bill Thomson), Bunny (Tommy Forbes) and Mr. Mole (Alan Melville, who subsequently went to London and greater glory). Another welcome visitor was Roland Smith who, as an 'aul' wifie', could equal Harry Gordon at his best.

The Aberdeen Animals indulged in typical children's adventures as illustrated in song and story. We also did plays, variety shows and had our own Concert Party, which we called 'Four-footed Follies'. Most of the material for this was written by Alan Melville.

This was the time of the Scottish Children's Hour, in which we were deliberately and self-consciously Scottish, from our opening musical signature, 'Bluebells of Scotland', played by Ruby on the celeste, to our closing cradle song 'Wee Davey Daylicht' sung by Miss Mouse. One of our script-writers told me she had no kind of success with the material she sent to Edinburgh, until in a flash of inspiration, she added the words 'Based on an old Highland legend' on the title-page. Thereafter, she couldn't go wrong!

The BBC staff in Belmont Street were a friendly lot. There was only one member with whom I was not immediately on friendly terms. This was Miss Jamieson who looked after contracts and bookings. She and I behaved to each other with a polite but icy reserve. As so often happens, this was to prove the basis of a much more lasting friendship than if we had rushed into each other's arms on sight. One day, before the ice was broken, she silently handed me a list of songs, submitted by a female singer for recital. This was the sequence of titles, 'Last May a Braw Wooer', 'I'm Ower Young tae Mairry', 'Doun the Burn, Davie Lad', 'He's Aye Kissin' Me', 'Hush-a-ba Bairnie'! We looked at each other, and then exploded into snorts and giggles. After that, we were friends for life.

She tended to dismiss as 'trashy' the light music I often played in gramophone interludes and, on her advice, I listened to Respighi's colourful 'Fountains of Rome'. "Why don't you give your listeners a treat for a change and play that?" she demanded. I did. The response was immediate. One anonymous post card which simply said, "Whoever selected that trash in to-day's record interlude should be taken out and shot!"

It was Moultrie's policy to mount at least two and often three original productions from Aberdeen each week. He kept emphasising to me the importance of bringing work to Aberdeen and the Aberdeen broadcasters. So far as actors and writers were concerned, he depended on a relatively small number of thoroughly experienced people. Chief among them was undoubtedly Arthur Black, who was well established as a script writer and actor long

31

before my arrival in Aberdeen, and his influence was considerable. I had been apprised of this before leaving Edinburgh, and I was somewhat apprehensive as to how he would react to a new broom, which if not actually in a position to sweep clean, was nevertheless likely to poke into dark corners. I need not have worried. From the beginning, Arthur Black was invariably helpful and kind to the newcomer, without the slightest hint of self-seeking. He wrote many scripts which I produced, but his most notable creation was a delightful radio character called Alexander Spinnle Shanks, whose initials were the key to his behaviour! Spinnle Shanks kept a diary of comical comments on the topics of the day, suggesting absurd remedies for the world's ills. The part was played by a dear old man called Willie Meston, whom we all loved.

Next to Arthur Black, the most prolific contributor to Aberdeen's programmes, both as a writer and actor, was George Rowntree Harvey. George had a lifelong love of the theatre and its players and a wonderful capacity for reminiscence and humorous anecdote about theatrical folk.

Aberdeen was full of talent in those days. There was Addie Ross, whose range, both as an actress and as a singer has in my experience been surpassed by one person only, namely Violet Carson. There was A. M. Shinnie, one of the earliest BBC announcers, a fine character actor and a most amiable gentleman. Other names that leap to my mind from out of the past include those of Dorothy Forrest, Betty Craig, A. E. Cruickshank, Laura Geddie, Enid Pinkham, W. M. Carnegie, John Foster, John Mearns, Grace Leslie, Louise Donald, Willie Kemp and a young man called Douglas Murchie, who was to become one of Scotland's most sought-after character players.

There was a young boy in short trousers whose name was Alan Munro and who was a most sensitive and conscientious young actor, and whose brother, Murray, was a wizard at sound effects.

One day, walking down Belmont Street, I noticed a very attractive young lady ahead of me. She too was making for the

ON MY WAVELENGTH

BBC, and by the time I reached the head of the stairs, she was disappearing into Moultrie Kelsall's office. "I wonder who that is?" I asked Miss Jamieson. "I don't know," she replied, "but whoever she is, yon's a girl with character!" And she was right. Her name was Helen Beaton, and she was unrivalled in the reading of verse, Scots or English. She was a gift to broadcasting. She and I became lasting friends, and many of my happiest memories of Aberdeen are of times spent at her home with her mother and friends at Argyll Crescent.

Another Aberdeen girl with whom I was on very friendly terms, was Ella Gordon Park. Ella was petite and vivacious, with lovely red hair and a beautiful complexion. She was a journalist with the Bon Accord Weekly and she wrote excellent BBC scripts. I produced a number of these including 'Byron's Boyhood', about the poet's early days in Scotland, and 'Eerie Evening', a somewhat sinister symposium for Hallowe'en.

Helen Drever was a dear little old lady, with white hair and rosy cheeks. She lived in Tain and wrote delightful scripts that were scholarly without being stuffy. She also wrote 'Ballad Days', faithfully reconstructed from the Victorian social life she had known so well. We kept up a friendly if somewhat erratic correspondence long after I left Aberdeen. This is one of her personally written Christmas messages to me:

'My Christmas Wishes'
I wish I were on yonder hill,
A-baskin' in the sun,
With everything I ought to do — DONE!
I wish I were beneath a tree
A-sleepin' in the shade,
With every tax I've got to pay — PAID!
I wish I were beside the sea,
Or sailin' in a boat,
With all the things I've got to write — WROTE!

HOWARD LOCKHART

Two other script writers who provided excellent programme material were Constance Charlton and Kathleen M. MacLeod. Constance Charlton, unlike some others, never claimed ideas based on legends, Highland or otherwise. She reflected the mood of the nineteen-thirties, with just a hint of the contemporary cynicism. Kathleen MacLeod, on the other hand, wove some beautiful scripts from Scottish poetry and prose, with titles like 'Sleep', 'Evening' and 'Springtime Serenade'. These scripts were pure radio, depending entirely on sound for their interpretation.

Remember this was a time when there were no recorded programmes. Everything had to be broadcast 'live', and the fact that something might just go wrong or that they might over-run only added to the excitement of radio in those pioneering days. One of the most original and ambitious of those broadcasts was called 'The Farm Year', produced by Moultrie Kelsall from a script by John R. Allan. I assisted by holding microphones and giving signals from strategic places in the byre, stackyard and the fields of the farm where the broadcast took place. Why a dark, winter night was chosen for this exercise I cannot now recall, but I know I did my bit wrapped to the eyeballs in scarves and mufflers to keep out the piercing cold.

John Strachan's farm at Crichie near Fyvie, where the programme came from, seemed exposed to the snellest winds that blew. There was, however, a compensating sense of excitement and urgency about 'The Farm Year' that generated its own warmth. John Strachan was a genial host and a 'natural' for broadcasting, with his fine, couthy voice and gift of expression. He was a fine singer of the songs and bothy ballads of Buchan that have provided such a strong, nourishing diet for so many Aberdeen home broadcasts over the years.

So, too, was a much younger man with fair hair and light, twinkling blue eyes. His name was John Mearns. It was not long, I may say, before I too fell under the spell of these tuneful and traditional accounts of rural life, like 'Drumdelgie', 'Barnyards O' Delgaty' and 'McGinty's Meal and Ale'.

There were others too, with many verses that would never pass the censor. At least, not in the nineteen-thirties. For this was a time of much more limiting censorship than we know in the more permissive conditions that prevail to-day. And if there are those among us who feel the pendulum has swung too far the other way, there is no getting away from it, we were forced into some very irksome and absurd restrictions. A comic script from Jack Anthony, that most endearing of Scots comics, contained a pun on the word 'bloomers'. This was quite unmentionable on radio. It was dirty. "What's dirty about bloomers?" protested Jack.

There was a song I often sang — heaven forgive me! — called 'The Wedding of the Three Blind Mice' in which there was the line, 'the preacher gave advice'. This had to be changed to 'the teacher gave advice'! (Apparently the clergy were not to be referred to in terms of secular song!). And, at the bit about having their tails cut off, where we should have sung, 'the bridegrooms came in their underclothes, they'd left their "tails" behind', we were forbidden to use the word 'underclothes' and had to say 'Sunday clothes' instead, making nonsense of the pun concerning 'tail suits'. But you see, underclothes were unmentionables!

Take the name Shand. Synonymous with Scottish Dance Music. But in the dear, dead days not yet quite beyond recall, it was Scottish Dance Music too, but not Jimmy — just Mrs. Annie Shand. She was a charming, elderly lady, who took me completely off my guard on the one occasion when we worked together in the studio, by presenting me afterwards with a box of cigarettes, "for announcing my programme so nicely". I was only too relieved I had got it over without the dreaded spoonerism which had overtaken one of my predecessors, when he announced, "Mrs. Band's Dance Shand"!

Mrs. Shand was, for me a link with earlier days. So was Violet Davidson. Nudging sixty, Violet retained a remarkably sweet,

35

strong soprano voice, and I loved to hear her reminisce about her younger days when she toured all over Scotland with her husband, David Thomson, a comedian, who started the Old Beach Pavilion, and gave first chances to an ambitious young comic called Harry Gordon. Violet also worked in concerts with Harry Lauder. Once he met her after an interval of some years and asked if she would like a drink. "That would be very nice, Harry," she said, with thoughts of a glass of port. But he took her to a dairy and gave her a glass of milk!

For BBC, Violet reconstructed her old-time concert-party under the title, 'The North Stars'. Among 'The North Stars' were Willie Johnson, a gentle tenor in the style of J. M. Hamilton, a great favourite with Scots of a previous generation; comedians, Dan Fraser and Danny Williams; Mr. and Mrs. Gus Stratton in domestic cross-talk; and the soubrette, Juliette McLean.

Juliette was a beautiful red-head, with a sweet voice and precisely the right suggestion of sauciness for a soubrette. She was a popular favourite in stage shows and concerts for many years. Returning from a concert in the country somewhere, she was in a car which overturned, and she has been a wheelchair invalid ever since, and a never-ending source of inspiration to all who knew her.

A motor-accident likewise tragically robbed us of one of radio's most original and creative broadcasters, Rab the Rhymer. Some of you, as you read, will recall the voice that sang, 'Oh I mak's them up and I sings them as I toddle on the road'. Then would follow a series of songs of social comment — always topical, always up-to-the-minute. The bearded rustic with the battered hat and pack on his back, as drawn in Radio Times, was a far cry from the man who was Rab. He was, in fact, Douglas S. Raitt, Doctor of Science, in an important government post. Small, dapper, always immaculately dressed, he was quiet and reserved, rather introverted and withdrawn. He was a regular broadcaster as Rab the Rhymer until his untimely death, his songs being packed with shrewd observation of character. His humour was invariably clean and wholesome. So was Harry Gordon's. In all the years I knew Harry, I never heard him crack an off-colour gag or tell a suggestive story, either on or off the stage. Good, clean fun. That was the Gordon comedy. At the Pavilion at this time, the Inversnecky period was in full swing, with Harry as the Laird. While other managements were reluctant to have their shows 'wasted' on the wireless, Harry welcomed the BBC and arranged his broadcasts to suit the unseeing audience. His preparation was meticulous. It was the same when he came to the studio. Every word was written down beforehand in his own handwriting, on margined sheets of ruled foolscap that he kept for the purpose. This procedure proved of special value to us when war came and censorship forbade the ad lib or unscripted word.

Harry's comedy being so clean and wholesome, he was ideal for Children's Hour in 'Inversnecky Bairns'. In later days, I worked with Harry even more than I did in Aberdeen, where he had the attractive support of his brilliant pianist, Alice Stephenson, as well as his accomplished 'feed', Jack Holden. But, on the stage, I always thought he was never better than in the Beach Pavilion, Aberdeen, where he filled the role of a benevolent father to the entire company.

Sometimes I was lucky enough to be invited to join them for tea on matinee days, when a long table was set up in the biggest dressing-room, and we would all sit round, with Harry presiding at the top. Happy days, ended all too soon when war came. Then followed for Harry triumphs in the south with his gallery of classic dame studies in pantomime, first with Will Fyffe and then with Alec Finlay.

At a memorial service for Fyffe, Harry gave the address from the pulpit. Quite suddenly he stopped. I looked up. This was no pause for effect. The tears were welling from his eyes. Walking home with me afterwards, "I don't know what came over me", he said, "I thought I had everything under control, but once I began to greet, I thought I'd never be able to stop".

Another time we were discussing his script in a hotel room in Dundee when rationing was at its worst. With an air of concentrated seriousness, he opened the door of his wardrobe and delved far inside. "Would you like a fresh egg for your tea?" he asked me with a mischievous smile. Would I like a fresh egg? I hadn't seen one for months. I have so many happy memories of my long association with Harry Gordon, and I have written and presented several radio shows about him. I shall always remember him with pride and gratitude. I am not ashamed to admit it — when I heard of his death, I wept.

CHAPTER 4

STARS IN MY EYES

IF Harry Gordon was the most painstaking of comics, then Dave Willis, at his best, was the most inspired. I knew him from the days when he was made a star by the enterprising Popplewell family at the Gaiety in Ayr. It is impossible to describe the qualities that made him unique, but unique he was. Never good at working from a script, his comedy was purely spontaneous and completely original. He had many imitators, he imitated no one. He could take the simplest of stories and make a ten- or fifteen-minute sketch out of it. The routine he called 'Mr. and Mrs. Biggar of Rose Cottage', for example, was just the old joke for children about baby Biggar being a little bigger!

I used to work with him in this sketch if we were doing it from a stage before an audience, and once I nearly wrecked it for him. About half-way through it, I had to make my entrance and interrupt Dave and his 'feed', Jimmy Plant. I made the entrance all right, but could I think of the line I was supposed to say? My brain went numb and I heard myself foolishly uttering the final, climax line of the whole sketch. It was a moment of sheer, paralysing horror. I can see Dave looking up at me, wide-eyed in disbelief. The pause seemed an eternity, when Jimmy jumped in, and with a deft twisting of the lines, got us back safely again and we finished the thing somehow. To his eternal credit, Dave bore not the slightest resentment, although he often used to pull my leg about it afterwards.

Of all the Scots comics I worked with over the years, the most endearing was surely Jack Anthony. We became lasting friends, and I have wonderful memories of Jack and the many, happy broadcasts we did together, usually with the amiable Bond Rowell, who in his own right was a first-class music-hall artist, and blonde, vivacious Bertha Ricardo. But at the time I first worked with him

39

in Aberdeen, his leading lady was a tall, dark beauty from musical comedy, Jean Adrienne.

Jack had one habit which I detested. If he knew I was in the audience, he would come down to the footlights, call out my name and invite me to stand up. Now I am never in the least reluctant to appear on a stage or on a platform, but it embarrasses me to be pinpointed in an audience. Once, during the war, Jack spotted me, came down to the front and began to bow and salaam in mock salutation, saying, "That's Howard Lockhart, my butcher. Must keep in with my butcher. Playing for bigger steaks!" I was furious . . .

Next day, I wrapped up a morsel of fat and gristle — meat rations were too meagre to waste more! — and sent it to Jack with a note which read, "Your butcher sends you your meat ration. Put it beside your gags and it'll soon smell the same!" Jack enjoyed the joke and, years later, he showed me among his souvenirs the note I had sent him with his meat ration. I, however, was taking no chances. When I went to see his show, I always stayed well out of sight!

It was in Aberdeen that I first met a luscious blonde called Nellie Norman, who played the ukulele and sang songs. I remembered seeing her as principal boy in 'Robinson Crusoe' at Ayr Gaiety. Later, as Helen Norman, she became 'feed' for Jack Radcliffe. One of the many qualities I admired in Jack Radcliffe was his boundless generosity regarding his own material. Most comics jealously guard their jokes and sketches. But in later years when I was producing the Boys' Brigade in their annual 'B.B. Fanfare', I knew I could always apply to Jack to give me something I could adapt. Once, in the Aberdeen Tivoli, I was announcing the programme from a very draughty corner backstage. When Jack came off at the end of his act, he apparently noticed I was shivering, for back he came in a moment and wrapped his warm sheepskin jacket round my shoulders as I continued my commentary.

ON MY WAVELENGTH

Jack was a born leg-puller and I remember one particularly hilarious tour of 'Workers' Playtime'. Anne Shelton was in the company and she too has a bubbling sense of fun. She and Jack were continually trying to score off each other, with Helen Norman, 'Ma' Shelton and me in the background somewhere. The fun was fast, but never furious. And it was — at least so we were assured — the sheerest co-incidence that at one factory the works hooter went off right in the middle of Anne's act! I must say, Jack had a very mischievous look when it did!

Nowadays when Helen Norman and I meet, we invariably greet each other with, "Do you remember that time when . . . ?!" Helen's uncle, Doctor Walford Bodie, was a top-of-the bill attraction for many years with his enormously successful act, which seems to have combined hypnotism and very clever showmanship. I never saw him on the stage, but he certainly convinced his audiences of his unusual powers. Once I went out to his home in Macduff to invite him to come to the studio for a broadcast interview. His house seemed to me large and slightly menacing, with its outside walls covered in seashells. Dr. Bodie was by this time an old man, but whether I imagined it or not, he had for me a slightly sinister air about him. He was, however, courteous and agreeable in manner, speaking in a surprising low and gentle tone. Magnetic, that was the word for Doctor Walford Brodie. Helen Beaton, who was in the broadcast with him, and was not exactly unaccustomed to appraisal and approval by men, told me afterwards she found herself dominated by Doctor Bodie and only by an effort of sheer will-power was she able to refuse his invitation to join him in his act at Blackpool later in the summer.

This was the time of the cinema organ, and, in radio, Aberdeen led the field in Scotland with weekly nationwide relays by Harold Coombs from the Capitol Cinema. In fact, the Capitol Cinema and the Beach Pavilion helped to put Aberdeen well and truly on the national broadcasting map. Although most of my broadcasting from Aberdeen was done from the studios in Belmont Street and, later, from Beechgrove, I always enjoyed outside broadcasts. At the Coronation in 1937, we did a concert from a hotel in Ballater on Royal Deeside and we did a documentary from the lighthouse at Girdleness. We also did a series from Dundee, called 'Dundee Discoveries', as well as a fascinating programme called 'The Tay Bridges' which dealt with the circumstances leading up to the disaster in 1879, and the rise of the existing railway bridge.

This was from a script by a Dundee lawyer, George Kinnear, based largely on memories related by his mother. She was a tall, lithe, sprightly old lady who remembered how, as a very little girl on that tragic Sunday in 1879, she and her brothers and sisters were hurrying home from Sunday School in the fury of the gale, which from time to time lifted them clean off their feet. Their combined efforts failed to close their front door when they got home, and they had to shout for adult help. One of the quieter scenes in the programme, contrasting with the dreadful drama of the disaster to follow, was also vouched for by Mrs. Kinnear. It related to the visit of Queen Victoria who was to cross the bridge by train soon after its opening.

On the way south from Balmoral, the royal train stopped at Dundee, where Her Majesty was presented with a bouquet by the little daughter of one of the town dignitaries. The donor of the floral tribute was a man of eminence in the city's affairs, but he had one pet economy. As a florist and greengrocer, he always insisted that the baskets in which flowers were delivered should be returned to him. When the child had dipped in curtsey and proffered the magnificent blooms to the royal visitor, the donor leaned forward and was heard to whisper magnanimously to Her Majesty in an undertone, "An' ye needna' return the basket, Ma'am!"

Not long after I came to Aberdeen, I was given the chance to meet one of my boyhood idols, Matheson Lang. He was one of the last of the great actor-managers, and his exploits in 'Dick Turpin's Ride to York' are still among my most stirring silent film

42

memories. Matheson Lang was to make an appeal in our series. 'The Week's Good Cause'. I must admit I was rather in awe at the prospect of meeting such a famous person, and I remember pacing up and down in the studio long before the actor was due.

At last he arrived, with his wife. In we went to the studio where Mrs. Lang unwrapped her husband from his long, capacious overcoat (it should have been a cloak!) and took his wide-brimmed hat. The actor settled down at the microphone with much elaborate business of changing from outdoor to reading glasses, and shuffling of script into a position that was comfortable for him. Tentatively I suggested he might like to run through it, and he readily assented. All was in order, and with a warning to him not to make script noises as he read, we awaited the red light. The moment it was out and the broadcast over, he turned to me with a hint of a smile and said, "I didn't rustle, did I?" I assured him he hadn't 'rustled'! And his wife began the reverse process of changing spectacles and getting him into his overcoat. Few words were spoken and these only in a kind of subdued hush. As she reached the top of the stairs, Mrs. Lang turned and bowed to me before starting down. The great actor followed her, then turned at the top step and looked at me. (If I had been shorter he would, I feel sure, have patted me on the head and addressed me as 'Laddie!'). "Thank you", he said, "thank you for your courtesy!" And with a swish of his coat-tails, he turned and went downstairs.

In 1938, I spent three months in London at the BBC's Staff Training School, where I cut no ice. I was bored by a lot of the abstract theoretical 'blethering' that went on, and I longed to be back at work in the studios again. All the same, I did enjoy being in London, even although it was at the time of the Munich crisis, and sand-bags and air-raid shelters were springing up everywhere. I was not sorry to get back to Aberdeen, and to embark on a new series called 'Nor-East Sidelights', which included a 'Visitors'

Book', in which we interviewed a famous person in the vicinity at the time.

One of our first guests was Tom Walls, who was on a fishing-holiday on Deeside. Tom Walls was famous as the stage and film partner of Ralph Lynn in the renowned Aldwych farces. He was also a figure to reckon with in the sporting world with a Derby win to his credit. He proved to be a delightful man, easy to work with. In the years immediately before World War Two, Aberdeen had the best repertory company I have ever seen. It was at His Majesty's Theatre, under the direction of A. R. Whatmore, a producer and writer of great ability and experience. His company included at least four names that were to become famous; Michael Denison and Dulcie Gray (very young, very newly-wed), Stewart Granger and his wife, Elspeth March. The Grangers, in particular, were in several broadcasts from Beechgrove that summer and I have lively memories of them both.

Vivid also, but for less happy reasons, is my memory of what happened with W. Fraser Simpson when he came to the studio. Composer of 'The Maid of the Mountains' and other popular music, he was an old man and rather frail by this time. Our interview was typed on script, and to accommodate one or two last-minute alterations we had agreed on, I had the amend-ments re-typed and pinned inside. In my script, one pin had penetrated two pages, which I unknowingly turned over together. When I asked the question at the top of my page, there was a deathly silence. Frantically, I moved to the next question further down the page. Still not a hint of response, just a look of blank dismay on the old man's face. Hastily, I swung round to be on the same side of the mike as he was, and to read off his script. When I came to the question I had already asked, I had just enough presence of mind to preface it with, "As I asked before . . ."

All went well after this, but the old man was thoroughly upset and insisted that the fault was his. I tried to explain what had happened and that the fault was entirely mine, but he obviously thought I was trying to make allowances for him — which made me feel even more of a heel!

Early in 1939, Herbert Wilcox brought Anna Neagle and Anton Walbrook to film sequences for "Sixty Glorious Years" at Balmoral, and promised to see me with a view to arranging an interview with Miss Neagle. On the morning of their arrival in Aberdeen, I left word at Beechgrove that I'd be back before lunch, and joined journalist Ella Gordon Park at the station, where large crowds were waiting on the platform to greet the celebrities. After the train drew in and official welcomes were made, we followed the entourage along the private corridor from the station to the Palace Hotel, where we all gathered in a room reserved for the occasion. Press reporters surged round Miss Neagle and Mr. Wilcox. Photos were taken. Coffee and drinks were served.

Ella and I were outside the central group and tried unobtrusively to edge forward. I caught the end of a sentence from Herbert Wilcox . . . "and I want Anna to have a rest and then we've a broadcast to discuss with the BBC". I moved forward and Mr. Wilcox shook hands with me as I introduced myself. He was small, neatly dressed in a conservative dark suit, and spoke in a quiet, gentle voice. "Anna would like to do this broadcast for you, Mr. Lockhart, so just tell her what you want". He then introduced me to the star.

I remember my impressions exactly as she turned and looked at me and we shook hands. I thought, "This is the loveliest person I've ever seen, the loveliest face, the loveliest smile, the loveliest voice". I was captivated. And not, as I learned, just a pretty face. A lovely personality. And, along the years these early impressions of Dame Anna Neagle have been more strongly confirmed.

We talked for a moment, and then her husband turned and said, "Excuse me, Anna dear, but I think you ought to meet so-and-so". "Of course, dear", she replied and to me, "Do stay and have lunch with us, Mr. Lockhart, and then Herbert and I can talk to you".

At lunch we discussed arrangements about bringing her in from Balmoral for the broadcast. Then we talked about the film and the prospect of her making a film about a Scottish character. Flora Macdonald was suggested. "We thought of that", she said, "but when I read it up, I found the legend of the romance with Bonnie Prince Charlie so exaggerated that we decided to drop the idea rather than falsify it. I have some fascinating books about Flora Macdonald. Would you like to read them?" "Very much", I replied. "Then I'll send them to you", she said.

Suddenly I heard my name being paged and, making my excuses, I rose and followed the boy to the phone. Who on earth could know I was here? And then my heart lurched and sank like a stone. I was due at the BBC to announce a programme! I had forgotten all about it. "They'll just have to go ahead without announcements", I told a distracted secretary.

Every announcer has a constant dread that, sooner or later, he will forget a programme and I was no exception. Now it had happened. In the event, the situation was redeemed, at least to some extent, by the resource of the accompanist, Miss Marie Sutherland, who, in her typically forthright manner, brushed all protestations aside and announced the programme herself. To this day, I may add, I still have a recurring dream, in which I am trapped in a lift at the precise moment when I am required to announce a programme!

A day or so later, we went to Balmoral, Ella Gordon Park and I, with Christine Crowe covering the visit for her paper, and Jack Fiddes as unofficial photographer. Jack was a medical student at Aberdeen University and one of my best friends. Alas! after graduating and working in a London hospital, he was killed early in the War.

The scene on the lawn at Balmoral showed Queen Victoria (Anna Neagle) and Prince Albert (Anton Walbrook) with the Royal Children in Highland dress. It took the whole day to film a scene that lasted perhaps ten seconds on the screen. Local folk from Crathie acted as extras, and there was much laughter and excitement in the air. During a break, I managed to see Anna and to arrange final details about the broadcast.

She arrived looking radiant, with her beautiful hair piled high on her head in the current fashion revived from Edwardian days. I was all togged up in white tie and tails, looking too terribly, terribly intense. I had a moustache in those days and took myself with all the deadly seriousness of youth. Looking at the photo, with the long, white pages of script dangling between us, we look as if we were the anxious parents of comon offspring, and for a long time after, friends twitted me about 'the christening photo'!

Afterwards, Anna invited me to dine at the Palace Hotel. "And of course, you'll bring Mrs. Lockhart with you" she added. I paused for a moment, then realised she meant Ella. "Oh we're not married", I asserted blandly, immediately aware of the implication. "Oh I see!" she continued with a hesitant smile, "Well, anyway, do bring her along". I did.

A few weeks after the broadcast, a parcel of books arrived for me, and with them a black-edged card which read, "Forgive me for being so long, but when I tell you that my father died shortly after our visit to Scotland, you will readily understand I had other things on my mind . . . Read them and return them at your leisure. With every good wish, Anna Neagle". Frankly, I had forgotten all about the books. She, characteristically, had not!

I also enjoyed a very happy social life during my years in Aberdeen, with frequent dances and private parties. I had done no stage acting since I left Glasgow and I was delighted when asked to play the detective in J. B. Priestley's 'Laburnum Grove'. This was for the Green Room Players, under the direction of an excellent producer, Tommy Forbes. It was also in Aberdeen that I accepted my first invitations to adjudicate and to lecture and both of these activities have proved lasting and profitable for me. But more of that in due course . . . Suffice it to say that in

HOWARD LOCKHART

Aberdeen I lived a full and busy life, enjoying everything that came my way.

Do you wonder then that I love Aberdeen with an abiding affection? Put to the test, I may say, when I returned twenty years later — as a TB patient. I was one of those picked up in Glasgow's mass radiography campaign in 1957. The knowledge knocked me for six! I couldn't take it in at first. I was to go to Tor-na-Dee within two weeks. "What are we going to tell the listeners?" asked Iain MacFadyen, who at the time was in charge of my weekly BBC programme in Glasgow. "Tell them the truth!" I said. And in my last broadcast, I addressed the patients in Tor-na-Dee with a word of warning. "I'm coming in beside you", I said, "come on — move over!"

My apprehension had visualised open chalets, scarlet blankets and waterproof covers to keep the rain and snow off the bed-clothes. All wrong! A delightful room centrally heated, with windows open no wider than for normal comfort. A glorious view of green grass, green trees and green hills beyond. In no pain, and with more than a streak of indolence, I lay back and relaxed. "How are you to-day?" the doctor would ask. "Comfortable and contented", I could honestly reply. Of the treatment, the consideration and the kindness, nothing but praise unstinted.

Visitors were always welcome, and here Aberdeen proved true to form. From twenty years back they came. Old friends with memories. Their visits, along with the letters, the flowers, the greetings that came from listeners, did more than anything else for my well-being. And out came the stars. Petula Clark came from Aberdeen by bus, delighted to be recognised by the conductress who had said, "You'll be Pet Clark. You'll be going to visit Howard Lockhart!" Pet, desperate to spend a penny, had to be rescued by a nurse from our all-male wing!

Frankie Vaughan had to face a queue of nurses and "up"-patients outside my door. Frankie, with fruit and flowers, on learning that one of the young patients being operated on that day was a fan of his, made a posy and wrote a card of good wishes, asking that these should be placed so that she would see them the moment she came out of the anaesthetic.

Ace trumpeter, Nat Gonella, was a frequent and generous visitor. He was doing a season in Aberdeen, and brought comedian Johnny Victory and the company, who gave us a wonderful show. I can never forget the kindness of the young singer, Gary Miller, who used to visit me on Sundays, and I was grieved to learn of his premature death within a few years.

And, of course, the Scots came out too — Gracie Clark and Colin Murray took us for runs into the lovely countryside. The Forest of Birse and the Brig O' Feugh were my favourite spots. Robert Wilson came, so did Kenneth McKellar, Chic Murray and Maidie, George Elrick, Jack Radcliffe and Helen Norman, Hector MacAndrew, and many others, not forgetting my BBC colleagues.

I was really happy at Tor-na-Dee. It was a happy place. The first essential was to relax and relieve the mind of worry. To accept the situation and not to fight against it. Soon I began organising programmes for our own closed circuit broadcasting system. We had panel games, we had quizzes, we had discussions. We even had plays. And, of course, lots of record programmes. I was also able to introduce a regular inter-denominational religious service on Sundays. And it was in Tor-na-Dee, that I became fired with the idea of providing a BBC programme specially aimed at hospital patients and those who are "shut-in".

I remained in Tor-na-Dee for nearly a year. In the long run, the experience did me nothing but good. But that was all in the remote future. I recall days of sunshine only in that golden summer of 1939. We even had rehearsals on the lawn at Beechgrove. And yet we lurched from one sickening crisis to another over Danzig and the Polish Corridor, names that I dread even to recall. It was a time of nightmare, with ever-lengthening shadows. One day, the Aberdeen Animals were rehearsing. Next day word came that the broadcast was off. The BBC was moving into the new attenuated pattern of what was to be wartime broadcasting. Goodbye for ever, Miss Mouse. Goodbye, Granny Mutch, Howard the Hare and the rest of you. Farewell, Aberdeen Animals . . .

Violet Davidson, on her way to the studio for "The North Stars" was buttonholed by a friend, who exclaimed in a Torry accent of fear and bewilderment, "Isn't it affa? They're boomin' Warsa'!" Violet laughed at the caricature of her tone. I laughed with her, but our laughter was hollow.

Rehearsals started. Violet singing 'Look for the Silver Lining'. A phone call from Edinburgh. The programme's cancelled. We can all go home. No one knows what to say. Then Violet, bless her, with memories of an earlier war, says, "Let's go and have a drink and a jolly good meal!" So to the Caley Hotel we troop. A bit sick, perhaps, and without much appetite. We had our meal, though. Plenty of butter, of course, and steaks and lovely white bread, and rich sweets for dessert, with lots of sugar and fresh cream. I hope we made the most of the feast before the fast. I honestly don't remember. But I do remember the new darkness as we emerged on to Union Terrace. The black-out had begun.

"Look for the Silver Lining", dear Vi, for it's all the light we'll have to steer by for a long, long time . . . Next day in the Control Room at Beechgrove, I heard Mr. Chamberlain's sad voice. War had begun. My Aberdeen chapter had ended.

CHAPTER 5

WARTIME BROADCASTING

I SEEMED to spend most of my time, during those first wartime days, in the Control Room in Aberdeen. No programmes were going out from our studios, so there was nothing for me to do. I believe I rather pointlessly started to index some music, but there was no future in it. Just a time-killer. There were constant cups of tea in the Control Room, and even an abortive attempt to teach me 'chatty' bridge! It was all so crazily abnormal, with everyone trying so hard to be casual. Some of us had to stay in Beechgrove at nights for a while — don't ask me why! — and we slept on camp beds behind rows of amplifiers.

And then, after the first few weeks, we began to adjust to the new way of life. Catriona Scott, one of Aberdeen's ablest young actresses, started up a concert-party called 'The Spots of Bother', and asked me to join. We did a number of shows, mostly at hospitals and institutions, and their very simplicity and amateurishness seemed to suit the mood of the times. Then I produced for Tommy Forbes and his Green Room Company, a play called, 'Sixteen', and this proved a very happy and enjoyable experience. We did the play in the University Union, and, as a result, I was asked by the University Dramatic Club to do a production for them. I chose 'The Torchbearers', a very funny satire on amateur theatricals. One of the students who took a leading part was Alexander Scott, now prominent in Scottish university and literary circles. After 'The Torchbearers' was safely launched, I was transferred back to Glasgow.

When I returned there, early in 1940, I found many changes in the BBC. For one thing, there was now a new Broadcasting House, further west, at Queen Margaret Drive. It had been the former home of the Bell brothers, all bachelors and all mysoginists. They had, however, an eye for beauty in art, if not in women, and their house made a tasteful setting for the many objets d'art which they collected. Ironically, when they died, their home became an exclusively female establishment, as Queen Margaret College for girls, in the days before co-education. The BBC were the next tenants, and they moved in during the late nineteen-thirties.

With the War, the staff was greatly reduced, and we were all likely to find ourselves doing things far beyond our normal range of work. I have a vivid recollection of helping Christine Orr to serve out breakfasts of scrambled eggs — ersatz, no doubt (this was a word in very common currency at the time!). Outside, we carried our gas masks dutifully, and gates and entrances were closely guarded, no one being admitted without a pass and identity card. As members of staff, we also wore badges. In the early months, when the sirens sounded, we trooped into Studio One, carrying our gas masks, but this practice was gradually dropped, and quite soon the BBC Scottish Orchestra needed Studio One when it was transferred permanently to Glasgow.

I was in the L.D.V. (Local Defence Volunteers), later the Home Guard, and I used to find myself on duty with Eric Roberts, one of the violinists in the Orchestra, trudging round and round Broadcasting House, our gas masks slung over our shoulders, rifles at the ready! But no ammunition! What we were supposed to do in the event of enemy attack, I cannot imagine! But march round and round we did, Eric and I, during that summer of 1940, usually pausing for a chat and a gossip behind the rear wall, overlooking the tennis courts and bowling greens above the River Kelvin. From the front of the building we could observe the position of the barrage balloons. It was Robert Dunnett who used to say —

"When the balloons are high, keep your eye on the sky;

When the balloons are low, no fear of the foe!"

Officially, I was now an announcer again, but I did a lot of producing too, especially when the Forces Programme got going. In the field of drama, many new artists had come into prominence since my days at Blythswood Square, including one of the greatest of all radio actors, James MacKechnie. Others included Eileen Herlie, Molly Weir, Maud Risdon, Eddie Fraser, Willie Joss, David Steuart and Eric Wightman. But I was mostly concerned with Variety programmes, modest ones to be sure, for our budget was strictly limited, and our supply of artists confined to those whose fees were within our range, and who were available at the time of the broadcast, recorded programmes being still practically unheard-of. I began to build up a rota of hard-working, capable performers, thoroughly experienced in their professional stage work, and who became regular broadcasters.

One of the foremost of these was undoubtedly Doris Droy. She and her husband, Frank, indulged in domestic sketches, simple and even crude, but vivid and laughable. Contrary to the raucous, stair-heid type of humour they used in their act, Doris Droy was a soft-spoken and retiring person, modest to the point of self-effacement. Her husband Frank, hen-pecked in the sketches, was, in fact, the dominant partner. During the War years, they played in the Queen's Theatre pantomimes with Sam Murray, another great comic, and played to packed houses at the Empress (later to become Jimmy Logan's Metropole). Doris was at her peak of success in the early nineteen-forties, when her ebullient personality, battling against adversity, appealed greatly to her audiences, whether on stage or radio. She introduced at least two catch-phrases widely used by Scottish servicemen at the time. One was 'Nae hairm done!' and the other, 'My hert's roastit!', the latter surely much more picturesque than a heart that is simply broken.

During this time, one of my closest friends was Gordon Jackson, eminent now as one of our finest actors. He and I loved the music hall and went to all the shows. One night we were at the Empress watching Jack Short and May Dalziel, father and mother of the Logan family. Suddenly, in the middle of a camp-fire scene, we noticed what looked very like real smoke curling up in wisps from the crude stage-fire, which consisted of an electric-bulb clearly visible beneath some red 'jellies', with a flex indifferently concealed.

May was singing in her full contralto beside the fire, when she became aware of the rising smoke. The singing stopped, there was a momentary pause, and then in perfectly audible tones, we heard, "My Goad, the fire's on fire!" The scene ended with 'nae hairm done', but a new catch-phrase was born that night — 'the fire's on fire!'

Married couples on and offstage were common at the time. In addition to Frank and Doris Droy and Jack Short and May Dalziel, we had Ellis Drake and Jack Fraser, Tom Cable and Dot Carr, and another couple, who, in the future were perhaps to be the best-loved of the lot — Gracie Clark and Colin Murray. But at the time I am speaking of, they did songs at the piano. Other comics I recall working with on many different occasions were Ike Freedman, a splendid Jewish comedian with an endless repertoire of funny stories and all suitable for broadcasting and our rather strict censorship. Pete Martin, most genial of men, and Charlie Kemble who specialised in making up impromptu rhymes about his audiences. He was often partnered by a delightful and vivacious lady who emphasised her considerable embonpoint with a song called, 'Nobody Loves a Fat Girl' ('but oh! how a Fat Girl Can Love!'). Her name was Maie Wynne.

Other performers from these early war years included Edith Thomson (formerly of The Thomson Sisters, favourites at the Princess's pantomime for years) — Elsie Kelly, with her accordion, and her song, 'Pistol-Packin' Momma'! — Cathie Haigh, in songs at the piano — and Janette Adie in a song about 'the domiciliary edifice erected by John' in other and simpler words, 'The House that Jack Built'.

During the summer of 1940, I found a whole lot of promising broadcasting material in the show at the Edinburgh Royal, with a cast including Jack Anthony, Bond Rowell, Bertha Ricardo, the Henderson Twins and Dickie, Robert Wilson, Ann Drummond-Grant, and Bob and Alf Pearson. There was always an air of quality about the Theatre Royal in Edinburgh, personified by

54

ON MY WAVELENGTH

Bumper Wark, the house manager in full evening dress, silk topper and pointed waxed moustache. As for the cast, this was the time when Robert Wilson was just approaching the peak of his popularity and he was well-partnered in duets with Ann Drummond-Grant of the Doyly Carte Opera Company. Bob and Alf Pearson were always top favourites in harmony songs. As for the Henderson Twins, who were impossible to tell apart, they were delightful in the family act they did with their younger brother, destined for fame as Dickie Henderson. The girls were always dressed identically and in the smartest clothes, so that people stopped in Princes Street that summer just to look at them.

Jack Anthony and his kind and hospitable wife, Carrie, had taken a house in Newington for the summer, where I often found myself a guest. One evening, when I called in at Jack's dressing-room at the Royal, he was on stage, and there were two young Army officers sitting talking to the Henderson Twins, who were just waiting to go on. At the end of the show, with other members of the company, we all trooped back to Jack's house at Newington for supper. The night wore on, and eventually Jack took me aside and, in a whisper, asked if my friends had any arrangements about where they were going to stay. "What friends?" I queried. "These two young subalterns", said Jack. "But I don't know them from Adam", I wailed, "I thought they were **your** friends!" Carrie was consulted, then the Pearsons and the others from the show. And no one knew them. In due course they left. They had behaved impeccably and we had all enjoyed the evening. The mystery was not solved until the next night, when the stage door-keeper explained they had called, asking if they could meet Jack Anthony and they were directed to Jack's dressing-room, where the Henderson Twins were waiting.

It would be pleasant to recall a thrill of pride when my age group was released by the BBC for call-up. It would be pleasant, but untrue! I was frankly terrified at the very thought of military service. But, like most other people in similar circumstances, I

55

assumed a superficially stoical acceptance of events I was powerless to influence. I was lucky in one respect at least — the BBC would make up my salary, so I would not lose financially.

With as few goodbyes as possible, I quietly slipped away from Broadcasting House, Glasgow, to begin a new life in the Royal Artillery. Before I did, however, I met John Gielgud. He came to the studio to make an Appeal for the Week's Good Cause, and I happened to be the lucky announcer. He was touring at the time with Beatrice Lillie in a miscellany of sketches and playlets, proving as successful in comedy as he was in drama. He proved also to be a wonderful talker, using his beautiful voice in rapid speech, as the thoughts of his agile brain tumbled from his lips. And what a modest man about his own achievements and ever generous in praise of others. He took me out for meals and generally showed me great kindness and generosity, realising I was unhappy and apprehensive about my forthcoming transfer to a military regime. "At least you'll be all right for theatre at Hereford Barracks", he said, "we played our show there just a few weeks ago". The reassurance had an unexpected sequel "Anyone here know anything about the stage?" bellowed the sergeant. "I do", was my immediate response. "Then take that bucket and brush and go and scrub it!" was the retort. And I did!

Army life did not come easily to me and did my health no good. And yet once again I was lucky for, after initial training and 'square-bashing' at Hereford, I was soon transferred to the Concert Party and Dance Band unit of Northern Command at Scunthorpe. And this gave me stage experience of a kind that proved invaluable and unique. Our show had to be such that we could do it in a 'super' cinema or on the back of a truck. Adaptability was the watchword. And I 'fed' the comics, played in sketches, sang and even danced! And sometimes I was just a chorus-boy. But in the main I had to write and produce the shows.

It was a source of surprise and disappointment to me that radio broadcasts by our Scots comedians meant so little to the Englishmen in our company. Until one day we heard the expression 'Oh! the size of it!' used by a comedian in the manner of an adult commenting sceptically on the precosity of an assertive child. It was because the boys in our show enjoyed his act so much that I remembered this comic's name. It was Alex Munro. On my return to 'Civvy Street', I sought him out and he became a prolific and popular broadcaster in our programmes. Alex is the father of screen star, Janet Munro, and he and I became the best of friends. My height contrasting with his short, stocky build, I was a useful 'feed' for him, and we got on so well together that there was a time when I was sorely tempted to accept his offer and leave the BBC to work with him permanently, by 'feeding' him in the act and as his manager offstage.

Our Army Concert Party gave many broadcasts, some from the studio in Leeds, and others from camp sites. This was in a wartime series called, 'Private Smith Entertains'. And I was invited to go to Bristol to do a record programme for producer, Frank Gillard, in his series, 'Forces' Choice'. I can't pretend I ever liked the Army, but the experience did me a lot of good, insofar as it broadened my outlook and widened my experience in entertainment. Looking back now my memories are entirely nostalgic and heart-warming, and I am often filled with a longing to see the boys in the show again, to revive memories of our peripatetic concert-party.

Back in 'Civvy Street' again, I was packed off to the BBC in London for a refresher course. London was not the healthiest place to be in, during the early nineteen-forties. To my delight, I found on arrival at my hotel that Nell Ballantyne was also staying there. Nell was an old friend from the Scottish National Players, and in her company it was impossible to feel depressed. Much of my leisure time was spent in her company and that of Gordon Jackson.

On my return to Glasgow, one of my first assignments was to produce the Morning Exercises with Coleman Smith and May

Brown. They were both experts in that particular field and their ease and style at the mike soon won them many admirers. Coleman Smith had also a fine singing voice and after giving detailed instructions for performing each exercise, he would join in the music and sing, "And DOWN with a BOUNCE and a BOUNCE!!" People liked to hear him singing, and this became so much part of the performance that sometimes the exercises were chosen to fit the music, rather than the other way round! I had to put myself through all sorts of contortions in choosing exactly the right tunes and ensuring that they were suitable for each exercise. As it was a daily programme, we had to change the music and have several tunes available. So the sheer physical effort in finding them was considerable. I used to go back to my office after rehearsals, panting, my braces dangling and my hair flying!

We got lots of letters and all the evidence seemed to indicate that the exercises were enjoyed and easy to follow. All the same, I couldn't help thinking my mother's reaction was probably typical. She followed the programme every morning in the bathroom, before going down to prepare the wartime breakfast. "I like the music", she said. "Yes, but can you follow the exercises quite easily?" I queried. "Oh these!" she said dismissively, "I never do **your** exercises. I just do my own!"

Another programme for which I was responsible was 'Scottish Half-hour for Overseas Forces'. This was broadcast in our Overseas Service and after the War it was re-titled 'Scottish Magazine' and ran for many years under the capable direction of Bill Meikle. For the Forces, we chose middle-aged maturity in our chief presenters. One of these was James Sloan. He had been in the earlier War and he sounded friendly and rather avuncular in manner. At the end of each edition, he used to say, "Roll On the Big Ship", a phrase that had been much used in the first War to indicate the troop ship bound for home.

The other presenter was Mrs. Helen Mitchell, who had played as Granny Ferguson in the Knockendoch series which she had

Howard Lockhart at home in his record library.

Harry Gordon.

Sir Harry Lauder.

Opposite:
Renée Houston.

Below:
Elisabeth Welch.

Miss Lillian Gish, star of silent films.

Our kind regards &
best wishes always
Howard!.
Sincerely
Stan Laurel.
Oliver Hardy.

Laurel and Hardy.

The Henderson Twins.

To our pal Howard
Keep cooking around to...

Gracie Fields.

B.B.C. Children's Hour on 5SC with Kathleen Garscadden.
('Uncle Alec'—2nd left, back row; 'Uncle Mungo'—3rd left,
back row).

'The McFlannels'.

JACK ANTHONY.

Jack Anthony.

Above:
Claude Dampier
and Billie Carlyle.

Opposite:
Henry Hall.

To Howard.
Hope the relay wont be
too Bad.
Thank you.
Charlie Kunz.

Charlie Kunz.

The author with Greer Garson.

*Michael Wilding, Anna Neagle, Herbert Wilcox and
Howard Lockhart.*

The author with Dean Martin and Jerry Lewis. On the right is producer David Pat Walker.

Left: With Barbara Mullen.

Below:
Broadcasting at Tor-na-Dee Hospital, Aberdeen.

Wilfred Pickles.

Gordon 'Tarzan' Scott.

Vera Lynn.

The author.
Above: At Queen Elizabeth's School in Hong Kong.

Above:
In concert party.

Opposite:
Adjudicating.

The author with Donald Peers.

written and in which I played as a child actor. She had a lovely, soft Dumfries-shire tongue and warm sincerity. We called her 'Mrs. Ferguson'. She had, in fact, a grown-up son in the army overseas, and he was able to report back to us regarding reception of our programmes.

In 'Works Wonders' we had a regular series of programmes of amateur talent from the wartime factories. This meant a great deal of preliminary work on my part in visiting works all over Scotland, in an endeavour to find those with sufficient talent to sustain a broadcast. It was at an aircraft factory in Prestwick that we first discovered a young man in his teens with a fine bass-baritone voice and a pleasing personality. His name was Alistair McHarg. But auditioning usually meant listening for hours to performances that were often indifferent. I sat, notebook in hand, jotting down my impressions, and very often one of the works officials would sit by my side. I deliberately made my writing as illegible as possible, being only too well aware of sidelong glances at my notes from the man by my side, a procedure which has no doubt contributed to the indifferent nature of my handwriting to-day! I also developed a kind of dead pan expression which remained stolidly the same, regardless of the pleasure I was enjoying or the suffering I was enduring. On one occasion, I was faced with a soprano with a most exceptional range of voice and a sound not entirely pleasing to the ear. My companion turned to me, saying in enthusiastic tones "Good, isn't she?" "I'm not sure", I pondered, "it's a freakish kind of voice". Nothing more was said but the atmosphere was chilly. I turned down that particular factory. A few days later, I was sent for by Mr. Dinwiddie, BBC Controller in Scotland. In his hands was a letter complaining that I had insulted the daughter of one of the works officials by saying she had "a voice like a freak!" Fortunately, I still had my notes, and it takes no great subtlety to distinguish between 'a freakish voice' and 'a voice like a freak'. But I learned my lesson and in future I was rather more discreet, and even more taciturn!

There were certain London-based shows for which I was responsible when they came to Scotland. One of these was 'Shipmates Ashore', a programme for the Merchant Navy, presented with much warmth and bonhomie by Doris Hare ('love from Doris'!). We did one edition, I remember, from the Merchant Navy Club in Glasgow. Doris Hare came up to be with us and the cast included Will Fyffe, who flatly refused to accept his fee and handed it over to the Club funds.

Another was the successful 'Have a Go' with Wilfred Pickles and 'Mabel at the table'. At that time, their travelling pianist was Miss Violet Carson, who was brilliant at improvising exactly the right tune to fit any given personality or situation. I must say I thought Violet Carson the outstanding feature of the show, although Wilfred has, of course, his own particular brand of genius. I foolishly elected to take the company to do a show in the Union to an audience of students in Glasgow University, forgetting their reputation for rowdiness. Normally, Violet entertained audiences in the hall, while Wilfred and Mabel met potential contributors to the quiz backstage. But the students would have none of her. They shouted, they jeered, they threw pennies and toilet-rolls on to the stage. But Violet went straight on from one song to the next, regardless of the painful fact that she wasn't being heard above the din. At last, Wilfred gave her the signal that he was ready to take over, and Violet made an exit, no doubt to her own considerable relief. "If that had been me", I said to her, "I'd just have got up and walked off". "Ah yes" she replied, "but I knew if I did that, it would be to admit defeat which would have made it all the harder for Wilfred". Which was undoubtedly true. When I hear the expression 'a good trouper', I think of that visit to Glasgow University and Miss Violet Carson.

Once we did 'Have a Go' from the Town Hall in Ayr. Gordon Jackson was with us and afterwards, he and Violet and I went to Kilmarnock and saw Wilfred and Mabel off on the London train. We three were returning to Glasgow where Violet was doing a broadcast the next day. It was a bitterly cold, snowy night and we found to our dismay that there wasn't a train to Glasgow from Kilmarnock for hours. So we decided to find a taxi, and Gordon and I set off in search of one. Let Violet continue the story as she reminded me of the incident in a recent letter — "When we eventually found one — the driver was none too amiable — but what puzzled me was the tender care with which you got me into the car. I learned afterwards that the only way he could be persuaded to come was your story of a 'lady in a certain condition'. Gosh, it was a good job it was a dark night!"

CHAPTER 6

THE McFLANNELS

"TO commend the McFlannels to their friends is unnecessary; to their enemies unavailing. Mrs. Pryde's characters speak for themselves in their honest, pungent, racy, homely idiom . . ." thus wrote Andrew Stewart, as BBC Scottish Programme Director, in an introduction to the first published book of the McFlannels. Praise or blame, depending on your point of view, must be accorded in the first instance to Robin Russell, for having had the perspicacity to see the potential quality for radio in a first script by Helen W. Pryde. Mrs. Pryde, a Glasgow housewife, had been entertained by a talk on the wireless about a country flittin', and thought to herself from her own experience that a city removal could be even funnier. She wrote the talk, sent it to the BBC, and Robin Russell advised her to turn it into a sketch. She did. And it went on the air, sandwiched between bouts of brass band music, as the first of a series called, 'The McFlannels Rub Along'. Every character had the name of a fabric. The McFlannels were warm and durable, the McVelvets and the McSilks definitely superior, the McCanvases and the McTweeds of coarser texture. McCotton, McGauze, McPoplin — the device was inexhaustible. At one point there was even a Frenchman, called Michel Valenciennes.

Well, the McFlannels 'rubbed along' at irregular intervals until War came. Then, with propaganda well in view, they came back occasionally as 'The McFlannels in Wartime', with humour about rationing, the black-out, the Home Guard, etc. Robin Russell was now in the Army, and when I returned after being invalided out, the McFlannels were in the hands of an English producer. I remember being in the studio one day, during a rehearsal, when the producer was trying vainly to make something of the rich local dialect which was clearly beyond his comprehension. I writhed in silent frustration. But, shortly afterwards, he returned south, the McFlannels were given a regular Saturday evening placing, and I was made producer. I was to remain in charge of the family for eight happy years.

With John Morton as Willie, Meg Buchanan as Sarah, Jean Stoddart as Maisie, and Arthur Shaw as Peter, the McFlannels were soon compulsive listening for an ever increasing audience. The situations were built mainly round the four well-established principals, but there were others that became extremely popular. Chief among them were Uncle Mattha (Willie Joss), a born scrounger, with neglected adenoids and corns, which he insisted were "a terrible tribulation!"; Mrs. McCotton (Grace McChlery), with her genteel accent and bad grammar ("If I had of knew, I nivver would of came!"); Ivy McTweed (Molly Weir), the wee Glesca keelie ("Ach, yous is jist a fish-custart faimly!"); wee Ian McCotton (Elsie Payne), who could be relied on to misbehave in the most embarrassing manner; and Mrs. McCorduroy (Elizabeth Swan), the warm-hearted neighbour who bantered so easily with Peter ("Hello, Handsome", "Hello, Gorgeous"). Helen Pryde always maintained Mrs. McCorduroy, as played by Elizabeth Swan, was her favourite character creation. When A. P. Lee took over production after me, some excellent new characters were introduced.

Mrs. Pryde was a complex character, as she herself admitted. She once told me of a very strict, puritanical upbringing. Anything to do with the theatre was sin. Writing 'wee plays' for the wireless would have put her practically beyond redemption. Although she enormously enjoyed her work as a writer, and was not indifferent to the fruits of its success when they ripened and fell into her lap, nevertheless I always felt that somewhere she carried within her some small sense of guilt. An intensely religious person, and one who genuinely tried to practise what she preached, she missed no opportunity to belittle her own work. One story she loved to tell was of hearing a woman in a train saying, "Ach no! I nivver listen to thae McFlannels. They're that coammon!" And of the grand lady — echoes of Mrs. McCotton — who maintained with complacent self-satisfaction, "Two things I'm proud of. I've never been to Woolworths and I've never heard the McFlannels!"

For most of the time I knew her, she and her husband lived in the country, first in Laurencekirk, and then in a fascinating old house in Forfar called The Friarage. About once a month she would come to Glasgow and pay me a visit to discuss future developments for her characters. We always referred to them as real people. "How's Maisie's romance getting on?" I'd ask. "Oh I don't think she's able to make up her mind", she'd reply, "but Peter's got a new girl friend!" "But I thought he was going steady with . . ." And so our imaginations raced on, as the family's fate was plotted. Often, as a result of these chats together, something new would emerge. One day we were discussing the need for a foil for the voluble Ivy McTweed. "Would she ever get a word in edgeways?" I queried. "She'd need to be the echo type" said Helen, "but we've already got that — I'm sayin' we've already got that" as she imitated the repetitive Mrs. McPoplin. "Could you not make Ivy's pal just a giggler?" I suggested. "Who never says anything but just giggles" said Helen, warming to the idea. And that is how the character was born — Bella the Giggler, as played by Effie Morrison.

Helen Pryde was not one of those writers who hang over you at rehearsals, breathing down your neck and taking the actors aside for whispered colloquies in private. There was a mutual respect that bound us, and we both had a love for the McFlannels as character creations. Not that we always saw eye to eye. On one occasion, at least, I put my foot in it! It was over a script called 'Where There's a Will There's a Fray' about some old aunt of Willie's who had suddenly died, and of the reaction to her will by some obscure relations, out to glean what they could from the spoils. The script turned out at rehearsal to be too short by a few minutes and, not able to contact Helen, I sat down and wrote in some extra lines — sticking to the obscure relations as far as possible. The author was furious. She accused me of ruining her characterisation. But the incident blew over and there was never malice between us. In fact, I came to love the McFlannels and looked forward with relish to our Saturday afternoon rehearsals. First we practised the sound effects. I liked to have them fully prepared before starting to work with the players. I remembered how maddening I used to find it, as an actor, when rehearsals were held up endlessly to experiment with some piffling sound effect which should have been in readiness beforehand.

Once when Maisie was supposed to be wearing a gorgeous new evening-gown, I wanted something to convey the importance of the dress. So I phoned Jean Stoddart asking her if she had an evening-dress that rustled audibly. "I think so", she said, always eager to help, "Why? Do you want me to wear it " "No, not really" I said, "but could you just bring it with you?" She did. And simply carrying it over her arm in the scene in question, with the swishing noise of the garment, she added greatly to the situation.

Nothing was left to chance. Every detail was carefully worked out at rehearsals. 'The McFlannels' were often credited with being 'that like the thing' and, although this was precisely the effect we aimed at and hoped for, it was achieved only after the most meticulous rehearsal and preparation. It was the result of co-operative team-work from start to finish.

Looking back, I recall the joy of these Saturdays. The joy of concentration in combining with the team to make each episode as good as we could possibly make it; the joy, naturally, of sharing in its success; perhaps most of all, the joy of being together, for there was a strong bond of affection and regard among us. It was all too good to last. The rot set in so slowly and developed with so little outward manifestation over so long a period, that, like a disease, it was too late to eradicate it when it was no longer possible to conceal it.

It began with remarks made to me by Helen Pryde about Jean Stoddart. Not, please note, NOT about Maisie as performed by J.S. Jean was a person who tended to dress conspicuously and sometimes flamboyantly. She talked volubly and often rather loudly to anyone who would listen, and like most talkative people, she could also occasionally be tactless. In short, she was a person whose presence you simply could not ignore.

By contrast, Helen Pryde was self-effacing and quiet. She dressed conservatively, usually in dark clothes, and anything in the nature of exhibitionism was completely foreign to her nature. She used to say she was intimidated by Jean's hats, which, even to my masculine eye, did appear rather impressive, both numerically and in style! Jean enjoyed cocktail parties, being herself an excellent hostess, and this did not exactly endear her in Mrs. Pryde's strictly teetotal regard. In the early stages at least, Jean was blissfully ignorant of the baleful impression she was building up for herself in the Pryde eyes, and went on her merry way, laughing and joking with John Morton and Arthur Shaw, and confiding details of her domestic life in Meg Buchanan.

It is important to remember that, long before she appeared in the McFlannels, Jean Stoddart was much in demand at concerts as an entertainer in her own right. As her reputation grew with the success of the McFlannels, she would often arrive at a theatre or hall to find herself billed as 'Maisie McFlannel' instead of Jean Stoddart, and naturally she took a poor view of this. Helen resented it even more when she heard about it, which seemed to be pretty frequently, judging by the number of times she complained to me about it. In fact, it became a growing obsession with her, to such an extent that she wanted the BBC to insert a clause in contracts forbidding the cast to appear publicly as in any way associated with the McFlannels. When the BBC refused, she produced a document at a rehearsal to be signed by the cast in an undertaking to comply with her wishes on the matter of billing for public appearances. Rikki Fulton was in that episode, I remember, and he pointed out, gently but forcibly, that the last thing they wanted was to be billed under any other name but their own. He added that it was clearly impossible to guarantee this, when billing was supplied by organisers of concerts and shows. No one signed the document.

Being unable to fault Jean for her performance as Maisie, Helen began to search around for motives for writing her out of the script. She would marry her off and send her abroad, she said. I begged her not to do this, maintaining emphatically that the success of the series depended on the four central characters as the unifying characteristic. At all costs preserve the family unit, I used to say.

Before I left for Australia in 1949, I told Helen I hoped she would do nothing drastic to change the family situation while I was away. But I feared the worst, and it was really no surprise when she wrote and said she had definitely made up her mind to marry off Maisie and send her to America! Which is precisely what happened and, when I got back, was a fait accompli. Not only that, but a year or so later, after I had finally resigned from the BBC, she brought Maisie back home again — and the part was given to a different actress.

Some years later, on a BBC anniversary, the Scottish planners decided to revive half a dozen of the most typical and successful McFlannel episodes and I was invited to return and produce those I had handled in the past. Archie Lee, who had taken over when I left and who was devoted to the McFlannels, produced the remainder. When it came to casting, the question of Maisie inevitably cropped up, I was emphatic in insisting that Jean should play the part where she had done so in the earlier scripts and I was delighted when Archie endorsed this proposal. By a strange co-incidence, Jean Stoddart had in fact gone to live in America, but happily she was back home at the time of the McFlannel revivals and was delighted to take part.

It was like a family re-union when we all met again for rehearsal. The first rehearsals were for one of 'my' productions, and Archie Lee, with characteristic thoughtfulness, had left a box containing a corsage for each of the ladies, and a buttonhole for the men. When we got over the intitial excitement and joy at being together again, we started to work, and it was as if we had never been apart. We had a wonderful time, and, through it all like a thread, there was a very definite feeling of gratification that Jean was back again in her rightful place.

These revivals delighted former McFlannel fans, but brought few new admirers, and the critics were lukewarm in their praise. The truth is that the scripts were already dated, both in content and technique. It is a tribute to Helen Pryde's skill that she could capture, with uncanny observation, exactly the atmosphere of the time at which she was writing. The old episodes will no doubt be brought out again from time to time and will, I like to think, become classics of their day, worthy to take their place in the immortal company of such other fictional Scottish characters as Wee MacGreegor and Para Handy. And certainly there will be those of us who remember the McFlannels with affection and will continue to quote familiar sayings like Sarah's reproachful, "Willie, don't be vulgar!" and Willie's provocatively optimistic, "Ach cheer up, ye never died a winter yet!"

CHAPTER 7

TOP OF THE BILL

SEVERAL wartime programmes were so popular that they continued long after the War had ended, among them 'Music While You Work' and 'Workers' Playtime'. The former was a non-stop programme of light music, without interruption for titles. Research apparently showed that output rose and production increased to a musical background, just as cows can similarly be beguiled into yielding more milk!

'Workers' Playtime', on the other hand, was purely recreational. Factories for our visits were chosen by the Ministry of Labour, and, provided they were technically suitable, we usually accepted their suggestions. We used to do three or four a week, recording a number of midnight shows where factories were open overnight, and these were stored for transmission at a later date. There was always an air of excitement about these midnight matinees. We usually had three professional acts for each show, always being careful to leave time for audiences to participate in some popular choruses of the time, like 'We'll Meet Again' and 'Roll Out the Barrel'.

Bebe Daniels was our top of the bill attraction on one occasion, and I can remember accordionist, Elsie Kelly, saying in tones of incredulity, "Me on the same bill as Bebe Daniels, my mother'll never believe me!" Ben Lyon was absent and she was partnered by Claude Hulbert. Bebe was one of the most conscientious and painstaking artists I have ever worked with. I was sharing production with Bill Gates from London, and he and I, with Claude and Bebe, had script conferences late and long in preparation for the show. We all sat around a table, with copies for consideration, while Bebe sat at the head of the table, pencil in hand, ready to analyse every single line she had written. If a line or a joke did not evoke an enthusiastic response, it came out. Anything slipshod or second best was intolerable for Bebe Daniels.

Another time, we were at Dundee for a midnight recording, with Dorothy Ward in the cast. I had long admired her as one of the best pantomime principal boys, and at dinner that evening, prior to the show, I was delighted to find myself sitting opposite her. A lovely vision she was too, in a beautiful, low-cut evening-gown. Rationing was then at its most acute, and we were all rather impressed to find there was a choice of dishes. All the others ordered soup, but some little demon of self-assertiveness prompted me to strike out on my own and I ordered orange juice. When it was served, I took a generous gulp which promptly went down the wrong way. I opened my mouth for air, snorted, and let fly across the table. There was a stunned, frozen silence. Fortunately, I had missed the lady's face, but I sat transfixed, watching little droplets of orange juice dripping slowly into that gorgeous bosom. Gasping, I stumbled to my feet and fled. When I returned, my eyes still red and sore, I apologised for my clumsiness. Dorothy Ward has a sense of humour and dismissed the whole thing as a huge joke.

Claude Dampier did a unique double act with his wife, Billie Carlyle. Billed as the Professional Idiot, he was a well-meaning fool who, with the best of intentions, got everything wrong. He had a fictional lady friend called 'Mrs. Gibson' about whom he would regale Billie Carlyle. Once he brought a storm of criticism on his head for a remark he made when 'Mrs. Gibson' was supposed to be in bed with a cold. "Where are you off to now?" inquired Billie. "Oh I'm off to squeeze Mrs. Gibson's oranges!" was the straightforward answer. This resulted in complaints about alleged vulgarity. Offstage, Claude Dampier was often very like his stage character. Once when we were travelling to Fort William, he walked the whole length of the train, carefully wiping the moisture from the steamed-up windows.

One of my special favourites from these 'Workers' Playtime' days is Renée Houston. I love her self-deprecating candour. "I'm not as old as you think I am", she'll say to an audience, "I'm much older!" I also love her for her deep sense of loyalty to those she's fond of. Once this loyalty was exercised on my behalf. She and her husband, Donald Stewart, and I got on so well, and enjoyed working together so much, that I invited them to do a series under the title 'Rendezvous With Renée'. Ian Gourlay wrote a song with the refrain, 'Rendezvous with Renée, a date with a pal'. This prompted one lady critic to write 'No, Renee, I am NOT your pal' and she proceeded to lay the blame for a poor show fairly and squarely on my shoulders. Renée was furious. Unknown to me, she phoned the paper in question. In her sweetest manner, she said, "Please tell your lady critic, my husband and I are looking for a chambermaid — someone to do the dirty work and empty out the slops. We think the lady in question would be perfect for the job!"

Once in one of the many radio interviews I've done with Renée, I asked her if it was not the case that she and her sister, Billie, had a very hard row to hoe when they started to make their way. "Not at all, darling," she replied, "Billie and I had no talent, you know, just cheek!" And when discussing her other sister, Shirley, she once said to me, "Listen, darling, anything I can do, Shirley can do too — and do it better!"

I ran into her one day on the street and told her she was looking lovely. "When you get to my age, dear", she said, "you don't look lovely, you just try to look neat and tidy. But I'm glad you did tell me, for I've had a bit of a let-down". Apparently she'd been in a shop further down the street, "Two girls behind the counter were talking about me — I could see them looking at me, then exchanging a few remarks. Finally, one of them leaned across and said to me, 'Here, have I no' saw you some place?' " Immediately Renée wondered how these girls could remember her. They were too young to have seen the Houston Sisters. Maybe with Donald on the stage? More likely in some of her film or TV roles. So, with her sweetest smile, she said, "Yes, darling, it's quite possible you could have seen me". The girl looked at her for a moment, and then she said, "Oh aye! I seen ye at the Bingo!"

She has a shrewd eye for talent, has Renée Houston. Once she'd been at Ayr Gaiety, and after seeing the show, she said to me, "There's a girl in that show — what's her name, Donald? — she's definitely going to be a big star". The girl's name was Beryl Reid. Beryl was a great favourite with 'Workers' Playtime' audiences. And so was Stanley Baxter. At one factory, he had to make his entrance by coming right through the audience in full female get-up. I had just stepped up to the microphone to introduce him, when the audience caught sight of him in one of his bizarre 'dame' creations. There was such an almighty uproar of shrieks and laughter that I had just to give up, and, for once, Stanley went on unannounced.

Another big favourite with wartime workers was Tommy Morgan. He had a wonderful 'dame' characterisation as 'Big Beenie'. Once he complained to his partner, Margaret Milne, about an upset tummy. "I know", sympathised Margaret, "it's this wartime loaf that goes for you". "Oh I never eat breid", said Beenie. "No? What do you eat then?" "Toatht!" came the reply, in that deep husky lisp.

Tommy had a manager called Geoff, who loved the greyhound track, and one night, Tommy, on an impulse, went along on his own to pay his first visit. At an interval, he wanted a drink and went into the refreshment room. Just as he was about to order, he noticed Geoff with some pals further down the counter. "I'll have a small whisky, please", said Tommy to the assistant behind the counter. "Sorry" was the reply, "we don't serve spirits". "But that's whisky that chap down there is drinking", said Tommy, pointing to Geoff with a glass in his hand, further along the counter. "Ah yes", said the assistant in tones of reverence, "but you don't realise who that is. That's Tommy Morgan's manager!"

Once, when we were doing 'Workers' Playtime' from a rather remote factory, Adelaide Hall missed the train, and just when I was beginning to get worried, she turned up panting, but all smiles. "I hitched a lift on the back of a lorry", she said gaily. For our broadcasts, we always had to exercise great care over the pianos supplied, and, usually, for safety and to ensure quality, we hired them. Kay Cavendish had a reputation for being 'difficult' about pianos, as well she might be, for her act depended on a first-class instrument. Before she arrived, I wrote and told her not to worry. "I've managed to get just the piano to suit you", I said, "It's a small upright with only a few notes missing and the keyboard only slightly smeared with jam!" Kay has a sense of humour. She got her own back on me at the factory. "How can you expect me to play the piano when there are no towels in the washroom?" she complained. "Well, you've got a tongue in your head, haven't you?" I said. "Yes", she replied, "but I'm not a cat!"

Piano acts are much less common nowadays. But songs at the piano were very popular in 'Workers' Playtime', especially from artists as talented as Kay Cavendish and Florence Oldham. It always struck me as odd that, on records, Florence was known as the Radio Girl and, on Radio, as the Gramophone Girl! In either capacity she was a great favourite for many years, and deservedly so. I have on my shelves a number of her old 78 recordings, made in the nineteen-twenties, some of them, and the sheer artistry of her singing and playing scintillates still, through the surface noise and scratches.

I must confess that I had some very anxious moments when we did a show at Musselburgh. Wee Georgie Wood was top of the bill, with his stage mother, dear old Dolly Harmer. Also taking part, we had an impersonator called Bob Gray. For some reason, Georgie took exception to one of Bob's impressions — when Georgie looks at you with that screwed-up enigmatic smile of his, it's hard to deduce his feelings — "That impression couldn't offend anyone", I said. "It offends me!" he replied. "Either it goes or I go!" He wasn't pretending. As he himself said, "he was just the so-and-so who would carry out the threat". Feeling that I was being put to some kind of test, I went to Bob reluctantly, and apologetically told him what had taken place. "I don't want to ask you to change your act, Bob", I said, "but still less do I want to drive Georgie into doing something dramatic". We both knew that he wrote a weekly column for 'The Performer', which was the bible of the Variety profession. In other words, Georgie was a force to reckon with. A few lines in his column could make one look extremely foolish. To my intense relief, Bob Gray took the matter in his own hands. "I can easily change it", he said, and, to his eternal credit, he did. I wonder what I'd have done if he hadn't? Anyway, Georgie was mollified, and from then on, he and I have remained the best of friends. It's just worth mentioning that, in The Performer the following week, there were some very flattering remarks about me, in which the word 'tact' was included. I had evidently passed the test . . .

One artist we were always delighted to have with us was Betty Driver. Especially in 'Workers' Playtime' and similar audience shows. Betty was wonderful at breaking down the reserve of the dullest audience. For many years, she was featured in Henry Hall's Band, and, latterly was a bright star in her own right. She and I still keep in touch and nowadays I enjoy seeing her in the part of Betty Turpin, the policeman's wife, in 'Coronation Street'.

Mention of Henry Hall reminds me that I bracket him with Charlie Kunz as possibly the most genuinely shy artists with whom I have ever worked. Both, I may add, thorough gentlemen in their unfailing courtesy and good manners.

'Scotland's Gentleman' is how Alec Finlay used to bill himself. I include Alec in my gallery of great Scots comics in the tradition of Lauder, Fyffe and Gordon, all of whom he greatly admired. When Alec worked for me, he knew that sooner or later I would ask him to do his 'Kirk Elder' a rich gem of characterisation. He and I were recently returning from a recording we had just made at the wonderful Red Cross Home, King's Knoll, at North

Berwick, and we were so absorbed in our chat that we had gone miles off our road, before we realised we were lost!

I am glad to include Alec Finlay among my friends. Inevitably, when you work with people, there are some you like more than others. Among those people whose visits we always looked forward to were Elisabeth Welch, with her hearty and infectious laugh, and Edric Connor, from Trinidad. Both superb artists and fine people to know. Monte Rey is another good friend. Never very happy with an audience in the studio, he used to beg me to put him as far back as possible.

In the late nineteen-forties, I toured hospitals in the company of the Scottish Variety Orchestra, with conductor, Kemlo Stephen, Ian Gourlay and various artists, in a series called 'Appointment With Cheer', parodying the popular thriller series, 'Appointment With Fear'. On more than one occasion, we had with us a charming husband-and-wife team, Ted and Barbara Andrews. I have had reason later to recall a remark once made by Barbara during a break in rehearsals. "We're delighted with our eleven-year-old daughter, Julie", she said, "she's just a natural coloratura soprano".

There was always a lot of fun when Maudie Edwards was with us. She and I never stopped play-acting, usually with her as the nagging wife and me as the hen-pecked husband. It was all very silly and childish, and nearly landed us in trouble once. We were in the railway-station at Stirling, on our way home from a broadcast, playing up to each other in our idiotic way. She nagged me at the bookstall, she nagged me at the ticket-barrier, she nagged me on the platform. Whenever I made an effort to defend myself, she mowed me down with a torrent of nagging. Finally, as usual, the laughter we had both been holding back eventually erupted. Maudie turned away, shoulders heaving, her face buried in her handkerchief. At that moment, I heard a sympathetic male voice behind me. "If that were mine, pal", it said, "I'd give her a skite on the jaw! It's what she's needin'!" A fellow-sufferer, perhaps?

HOWARD LOCKHART

Regularly in 'Appointment With Cheer', we had a quiz on a variety of subjects relative to Scotland. 'Call Yourself a Scot!' we named it. Once I found myself towering over an attractive young nurse, who had elected to choose as her subject the meaning of Scottish words and phrases. "What", I asked her, "what is meant by the expression, 'a muckle chiel' ". Now every self-respecting Scot knows — or should know! — it means 'a big fellow'. But she clearly did not. So to give her a helping hint, I said, "Well look at me. You might say that I'm 'a muckle chiel' ". She gazed at me blankly for a moment, and then "Oh yes" she said, "a great, big hungry child!"

I can never claim to have been an ambitious person. I remember how shocked Beryl Reid was when I made that confession to her. But, while I was Variety Producer for Scotland, I did have one secret goal. I did want to work, just once, with the two top 'names' in the profession. At the time, these were Gracie Fields and Sir Harry Lauder. I managed to achieve both objectives.

At the end of the War, Gracie did a tour of the main cities in 'Gracie's Working Party' — more propaganda! — and we broadcast it from St. Andrew's Hall in Glasgow, with an orchestra of local musicians and a choir from — appropriately! — Singer's factory at Clydebank. The morning rehearsal went badly. Gracie seemed edgy and tense. After the mid-day break, I asked her if she had had a nice lunch? "Don't bother me with that just now", she snapped. I must admit to feeling somewhat squashed, but later that day, she very generously apologised to me. "I'm sorry, lad", she said, "but I've been a bit worried about this show". Evening came and we began. Instead of waiting in her dressing-room until it was time for her call, she paced up and down in the wings listening to the reaction of the acts that preceded her. As top of the bill, she was naturally last to go on and, as her entrance drew nearer, she seemed to get more and more agitated. At last curiosity overcame me, and, risking another snub, "You're not nervous, are you?" I asked. "I'm petrified!" she replied. "But this is something

I find very hard to understand", I went on, "after all, a star in your position — you have any audience at your feet". "Yes", she retorted, "but when you're on a pedestal, it's very easy to be toppled off!" It's just worth adding that, after the show, in which her triumph was never in doubt, she was a different person, totally relaxed and full of fun.

Two friends of Gracie's were in the audience that night, Sir Harry Lauder and his niece, Greta. By this time I had worked on several broadcasts with the old man, and knew him pretty well. Not that we exactly took to each other on sight at our first encounter. This took place in Jack Anthony's dressing-room at the Glasgow Pavilion. It was during the War, and I was in Army uniform. Suddenly there was a knock at the door, and who should come in, but Miss Lauder, followed by her uncle. In the chat that followed introductions, I heard myself making some rather disparaging remarks about Army life, half in earnest, half not. There was an icy silence, then, looking me up and down, the old man said, "And are ye no' proud to be fighting for your Country?" Then I realised I had been rather tactless, to say the least of it, for he had lost his only son in the earlier War. However, if I didn't make much of an impression on him on that occasion, he didn't exactly endear himself to me.

A couple of years or so later, back at the BBC, I was sent out to Lauder Ha' at Strathaven, to invite Sir Harry to do a 'live' broadcast on his birthday, which was the fourth of August, the birthday also of the Queen Mother (she was still of course Queen at that time). When I mentioned this to Sir Harry, he said, "Oh I ken. I telt her!" "What do you mean, you told her?" I queried. "I said to her, 'my birthday's the same day as yours, Ma'am. But I got mine in first!' "

I'm sure I must have implied to the old man that the BBC was bestowing something of an honour on him with the invitation, but he was singularly unimpressed. "No, I will **not** come to your studio", he said. "But why not?" I asked. "**Because** it's my birthday", he replied, "that's the night I have my party, and I'm not giving that up for any broadcast. Now do ye ken this song?" And, sitting at the fireside away he'd go into one of those tuneful songs of his. It was then, in that cosy little upstairs study, over tea and the flickering firelight that I first fell under his spell.

It was, at that time, still something of a novelty to record a programme beforehand, but, in view of the birthday situation, back I went to Lauder Ha' to offer the pre-recording. "So you want me to make a record?" he asked. "Yes, please" I replied. "Aye, well, I'm nae daein' it!" he said. "But why **not?**" I pleaded. "My boy", he said — he nearly always addressed me as 'boy' or 'my boy' — "My boy, when I made records, I made them for H.M.V., His Master's Voice. There was no contract, just a handshake, just a gentleman's agreement, but I gave my word. I'm no' goin' back on it now. Do you ken this song?" — and away he'd go again, in his lilting voice that never lost its pitch and rhythm, even when he was an old man. But it seemed as if, once again, I had failed in my mission.

When Greta was showing me downstairs on the way out, she said, "You know, Howard, I don't think Uncle realises that this is not a record for commercial purposes. But you leave it to me. I'll speak to him — at the right time!" Sure enough, next day she phoned to say that Uncle would be 'delighted'. That was perhaps the first, but not the last time, that Greta Lauder proved a good friend to me. She knew her uncle and she knew exactly how to handle him. The fact that she adored him did not blind her to the little faults and frailties that made him such an endearing old man. Such as his embarrassing habit of asking women their ages! And his pipe-smoking. She used to say, "Uncle, you just have one smoke a day. And it lasts from after your breakfast till you go to your bed at night!"

Once, after I had worked with Sir Harry in the studio a few times, I was invited to one of his birthday parties. And I may say

ON MY WAVELENGTH

I was one of the few people there not related to him. He had a strong feeling for kinship and he loved having his relations round him at such a time. Well, there we were, sitting in the big lounge at Lauder Ha', waiting to hear his recorded broadcast, when, from the radio in the corner, came the voice of Pamela Patterson, the announcer, wishing him a happy birthday. At that the old man got up from his seat, bowed to the loudspeaker and said, "Thank you, my lassie, that was nice!" Then the songs began, and we all started to sing, but this was not to his liking at all. "No, NO", he shouted, "not like that. Listen to the chap that's singing them. Like THIS!" And he proceeded to conduct us. He was having a wonderful time. And, of course, so were we! When the time came to go through to the diningroom for the meal, Sir Harry took me by the elbow and guided me across the hall to the seat beside him at the top of the table. "I want you to sit beside me", he said, to my amazement and delight. "Oh, thank you, Sir Harry", I stammered, "that's very kind of you —". "Oh I'm no' doin' it because it's you", he replied, "I'm just doin' it to prevent **them** from fightin' over which one of **them** is going to sit beside me!"

Not that it was all sweetness and light with Sir Harry. He could be 'difficult'. I remember one day in the studio when things had not been going well at rehearsal. Ian Whyte, the conductor, finally put down his baton and said, "Well, Sir Harry, I think we'll stop now and have a break for tea". There was a pause, then the old man glowered up at him and said, "There'll be nae tea till I've finished". Ian Whyte tried to reason with him, but no! he was not to be won over. It looked as if matters had reached a deadlock, when, from the background, always there, always unobtrusive, came his niece. "Now, Uncle", she said, taking his arm, "I'm sure you would enjoy a cup of tea and a smoke with Ian and the boys". He scowled at her and we all waited with bated breath. Then his face lit up and his eyes twinkled, "Aye, come on", he said, "a wee cuppa tea!"

HOWARD LOCKHART

Like a lot of old people, he had some small weakness of the bladder. Once he called me over during rehearsal. "Boy!" he shouted, "boy, come here, please. I'm needin' the lavatory, will you show me where it is?" In its wisdom, the BBC had no toilet on the ground floor, and one had to go either up one stair or down. To save him the trouble of the rather slippery staircase, I guided him into the lift. "Here, where are you taking me?" he queried, disengaging his arm, "it's the lavatory I'm wantin' ". "I know, Sir Harry", I explained, "I'm taking you to the one that's nearest". "Well you'd better hurry", he said, with feeling, "for I'm sair needin'!"

His recording sessions seemed endless because he was never content just to record the full programme and then do re-takes afterwards. Oh no! He would record one song, and then listen to it being played-back. And if he wasn't satisfied, and he seldom was, it had to be done again. I asked him one day why he was so painstaking. "My boy", he said, "When I went for my first trial — aye, you would call it an audition to-day — it was to the Old Scotia Theatre in Stockwell Street, where a Mrs. Bayliss heard me do my turn, and after I'd sung my songs, do you ken what she said? She said, 'Ach, laddie awa' hame an' practise!' And I've been practising ever since". And it was true, for Sir Harry was a perfectionist to his finger-tips.

Was Lauder mean? This is a question I am often asked. He loved to pretend that he was, and he certainly did much to perpetuate the myth of the 'canny Scot'. But he was never mean in my experience of knowing him. On the contrary, to me he showed a generosity of spirit that I never would have expected from what I had read and heard about him. Here are two letters he wrote me, in his own handwriting. When I was off work with a cold, he wrote:—

Dec., 26th, 1945. Lauder Ha', Strathaven.

My Dear Mr. Lockhart, Sorry you were off. My rehearsal went big and I do hope you will be well enough to be at studio on Ne'erday. I feel certain it will be a big success as always before. I trust you are in good fettle and hope to see you when I am on the job. May God bless you and keep you with us. We need you.

Yours sincerely, Harry Lauder.

And on the eve of my departure for Australia:—

Dec., 1948. Lauder Ha', Strathaven.

My dear Friend Howard, May I wish you luck on your trip to Australia, you are certainly worthy of success. My sincere wish is that the Australians will give you the same welcome as they gave me on my trips to their lovely country.

A' the best a' the time, Harry Lauder.

Some years after his death, when Greta and I had done a broadcast together about her beloved Uncle, she wrote:—

My Dear Howard, As I told you on the phone, I love to work with you, and so did Uncle. He always said after we left you, 'Howard is such a gentleman' . . .

Once, when she came to see me, she said, "I think Uncle would have liked you to have something of his, so I've brought you this", and she produced from her handbag a little silver notecase with 'H.L.' on the front. The co-incidence of the initials was the main reason for her choice. She had my name, 'Howard', engraved on it too. I kept it as a treasured possession, with the faint pencil notes, illegible now, on the faded, mottled pages.

Then a year or two ago, I took it, along with his two letters to me, and a large signed photo he once gave me — and handed them over to the curator of the small but attractive Museum at Hamilton, where there is a considerable collection of his stage props, costumes and music. And there they remain for posterity, as souvenirs of the man whom Churchill called 'Scotland's Minstrel'.

CHAPTER 8

PERSONAL CHOICE

A LTHOUGH I greatly enjoyed being the BBC's Variety Producer in Scotland, I did not want to make it my life's work, and, by the end of the nineteen-forties, I was unsettled. I had a desire to travel. I thought if I could get away for a while, I could do some personal stock-taking and have a clearer vision in which direction my future lay. And so I went to our Controller, Mr. Dinwiddie, and told him what was in my mind. I knew he would give me a fair hearing and good advice, and I was not disappointed. "If I were a young man in your position, I should probably want to do the same", he said. My idea was to get the BBC to suspend me without pay for a couple of years, and then take me back at the end of that time. Meanwhile, I would go to Australia and try to find work there, either on radio or the stage. If I didn't, I could afford to keep myself for the limited period. Mr. Dinwiddie felt the BBC would be unlikely to suspend me. "What you **could** do", he said, "although it would be a risk — you could just resign and go abroad. The chances are that, knowing you, and knowing what experience you had, we would very likely take you back again, if that was what you wanted". I decided to take the risk, and went at once to a shipping office to book a passage for Australia. More accurate to say I had my name entered for one, as just at that time there was a long waiting list. "It might be a year or eighteen months", the shipping people said. I was in no hurry, but relieved now that I had taken the decision.

Months rolled on. Then one day Mr. Dinwiddie sent for me. "Are you still keen to go to Australia, Howard?" he asked. "Oh yes", I replied, "I'm still waiting for a vacancy on board a ship". "How would you like to go out for us?" he said, with a mischievous smile. I could hardly believe my ears! "You would

82

have to fly out in three weeks", he went on. "You'll be attached to the Australian Broadcasting Commission in Sydney, but your salary and expenses will be paid for by us. Oh — and you'll be away for six months only!" he added. To say I was elated is an understatement. I was thrilled beyond words. Here I was, getting exactly the trip I wanted, without any risk to my position with the BBC — and getting paid for it too! Mr. Dinwiddie had clearly been working on my behalf behind the scenes and I have never ceased to be grateful to him.

Within the next three weeks, Trafford Whitelock arrived from Sydney, as the other half of the exchange, and I was off on a journey to the other side of the world. The outward trip was via Rome, Cairo, Karachi, Calcutta, Singapore and Port Darwin — where there was a telegram from the ABC welcoming me to Australia. On the return journey six months later, I flew via Honolulu, San Francisco, Chicago and New York, thus completing my first world tour.

Even now, all these years later, I find it hard to be coolly objective about my time in Sydney with the Australian Broadcasting Commission. I don't think there has ever been a period in my life when I was happier or more fulfilled. I loved my work, producing variety shows very much like those at home. But I was allowed wider scope and found myself involved with drama and documentaries as well. I produced my play about Madeleine Smith, both on radio and on the stage, and both productions seemed to go down well. I loved the people I was working with. They were enthusiastic, talented and so professional in their approach. Socially too, I was in my element among kind, friendly people who overwhelmed me with their hospitality. I worked hard in Sydney and I also spent a short time on programmes in Melbourne. To my regret, I never found time to visit Queensland, but I did manage a brief but enjoyable week-end on 'a station' in the bush in New South Wales.

And I did my stock-taking. I realised that I wanted to diversify my activities, in a way that would not be possible while I remained a member of BBC staff. I wanted to do more writing, more stage production and, paradoxically, more broadcasting. At the time, staff producers, if not actually forbidden, were certainly not encouraged to take part in programmes. No such taboo operated in Australia, which was one reason why I so much enjoyed working there. After much thought, I decided to resign and become a free lance. But, bearing in mind the generosity of the BBC in affording me the Australian trip, I told Mr. Dinwiddie I would not consider doing so for at least one year after my return. And so, in due course, having been a member of the staff for fifteen years, I resigned my job as Variety producer and handed it over to my successor, Eddie Fraser.

I was — and still am — grateful for these years, and I can testify to the generosity of the BBC to its staff. More important, the experience had been invaluable, and here I was, I, who had grown up with the BBC, about to break loose and sacrifice the protective arm of staff employment for insecurity. It was Anona Winn, who said, when I told her I was thinking of leaving, "Well you know, Howard, the BBC sometimes smothers while it mothers!"

Thus I joined the ranks of the self-employed in 1950. Let me say, here and now, that I have never seriously regretted it for a moment. True, at first I did have some rather depressingly lean times, but these never lasted. Bill Meikle put me into his 'Scottish Magazine' in a series called 'Stravaigin'' in which I described my experiences in different places at home and abroad. I got some work in Children's Hour plays too, and then I suggested the idea of a gramophone programme in which I should play records chosen by famous people in an interview with them. It was a kind of poor man's 'Desert Island Discs'. Where that programme gave a choice of eight records and one celebrity, we would provide a number of famous folk, each choosing one record only. The idea was accepted by producer, David Pat Walker, and it was he who chose the recording by the Melachrino Strings of 'Limelight' as the signature tune. I still use the same signature tune to-day. We called the series 'Personal Choice'.

I am not ashamed to say that I enjoy meeting famous people, if only to try to determine what particular quality they have that makes them outstanding. Not that I have been able to draw any very profound conclusions. I'd simply say that, in my experience, it is the 'big people' who do the 'little things' — the big people who show that extra little bit of consideration for others. Like Greer Garson, for example.

Sometimes I carried a portable tape-recorder and did the recording on my own, but, in the earlier days, these were not available, and we had to book the Recording Car, and park it outside. When Greer Garson came to Edinburgh, I went to interview her at her hotel. Gerry Girot was Recording Engineer, and he remained below in the car, while we did the recording from her upstairs suite. Like all the best artistes, Greer Garson is a perfectionist, and the recording had to be done over and over again before she was satisfied. In between each 'take', she heard me saying, "Right, Gerry, we'll go ahead again, Gerry . . ." When it was finally concluded, she grabbed the mike and said into it, "And now, I'd like to invite Gerry to come up and join us for tea, if he'd like to". He didn't need coaxing. The lady kicked off her shoes and sat with her feet tucked under her, as she dispensed the tea and sandwiches, regaling us with tales of Hollywood.

A few days later, I got a letter bearing on the envelope the crest of the Dorchester Hotel in London. None of my friends move in quite such exalted circumstances, so I was rather mystified as I slit it open.

"Dear Mr. Lockhart" — it ran —

"I returned to London after the completion of my tour and am now flying to the States this evening. Before leaving, however, I just wanted to write and say how much I enjoyed working with you and our Chum at the BBC recorded interview. Many thanks and I hope it was well received by your listeners. With very best wishes, Yours sincerely, Greer Garson".

At this stage I have forgotten the record she picked. But I do remember Frank Sinatra's choice, if only because it was so unexpected — any part of the 'Mother Goose' Suite by Ravel. He had the reputation of being a hellraiser and rather 'difficult' to interview, so I was a bit apprehensive when I went backstage at the Glasgow Empire. I learned that he scarcely used his dressing-room at all. He simply walked in and did his act for the first house, disappearing immediately afterwards into a waiting car, not being seen again until just before he was due for his second-house show. When that was over, away he went again. I stationed myself just inside the stage door and tackled him the moment he arrived for the second house. After a few moments of chat, his cue came and he went straight on to the stage. To me he was quiet, courteous and brief.

Sir Ralph Richardson also gave me a surprise. Not because of the music he chose, but because he couldn't choose any! "I have no ear for music", he confessed with his bland smile, "I think I might just recognise the National Anthem, but that's about all!" He was most apologetic and polite, but I left him having failed in my mission. But, in a day or two, I had a letter from him, saying how sorry he was for "being unhelpful". He then added that, as a child, he had been taken to see the Gilbert & Sullivan opera 'Ruddigore', and subsequently a record of the music had been bought for the family gramophone. I was to play for him something from 'Ruddigore' to remind him, as he so picturesquely put it, "of the music on the machine!"

Frankie Howerd's taste ran, he said, to Passacaglias and Fugues. I was carrying a light raincoat the night I called to see him at the Edinburgh Empire, and I hung it on a hook behind the door. We had exchanged only a few words when it was time for Frankie to go onstage. He directed me through the pass door into the auditorium where I stood at the back of the stalls, watching the show. As soon as he walked on to the stage, I thought the coat he was wearing was very like my own. In fact, I was sure it **was** mine! My suspicion was confirmed when, after a couple of gags, he took off the coat, tossing it on the piano, whereupon all the loose change I had in the pockets rolled down into the footlights. There was the merest fraction of a pause — I could almost sense his momentary stupefaction! — and then he quickly quipped something about — "Oh! they're paying us in coppers this week. Well, it saves a lot of bother really" whereupon he walked around collecting the coins. When I saw him afterwards, he explained that he always wore a coat at his entrance in that particular act, and he just blindly clutched mine from behind the door, not realising his mistake until the cash tumbled out!

When they visited Scotland with their stage double-act, Dean Martin and Jerry Lewis were enormously successful. In London their reception was less enthusiastic. I remember how thrilled they were with the response from Scottish audiences. Jerry Lewis kept taking snaps of them from the stage. I expect most people thought it was a prop camera, just used in the act, but he was in fact, taking pictures of the audience. They were both easy to work with, but, of the two, Dean Martin was perhaps the more conscientious about the interview we recorded. Jerry Lewis wanted to get back to his pictures. About Dean Martin, I may say, there was not the slightest hint of the 'drink' image which is now so much part of his stock-in-trade. I suspect that, like Jack Benny's meanness, it is a good gimmick for jokes about him, and is hardly borne out by the facts.

Another couple I liked enormously turned out to be remarkably true to type, namely Laurel & Hardy. Laurel was quiet and rather withdrawn, whereas Hardy was voluble and chatty, with that charming air of old-world courtesy and good manners so characteristic of his screen image. I can't now remember who was on the bill with Laurel & Hardy at the Glasgow Empire when I interviewed them, but I do know that a great many of the top-liners of to-day were frequently to be seen, usually in very modest 'spots'. Russ Conway used to accompany Dorothy Squires and other singers. Ken Dodd was a frequent visitor, and so were Max Bygraves, Terry Scott, and Morecambe & Wise.

One of the most delightful artists to meet was Nat King Cole, and one of the best-dressed. I remember remarking to him how much I admired his frilled evening-dress shirt, which was the first of its kind I had seen. "In a year or two, they'll all be wearing them," he said, "and then we'll have to go back to plain ones again!"

'Tarzan' was tired! Yes, Gordon Scott, in Scotland on some kind of promotion tour, was exhausted when he arrived at Broadcasting House. A charming man. he was most apologetic for hardly being able to keep his eyes open, explaining that he was on a very wearying schedule of engagements in a very short space of time. It was long enough, however, for us to do the interview, although we had almost to prod him to keep him awake!

Someone else on a schedule that would have daunted a much younger person was Miss Lillian Gish, now a sprightly lady in her seventies. She arrived in Edinburgh for the Film Festival, clutching under her arms two tins of film, containing excerpts from the great silent classics of the pioneer director, D. W. Griffith. In now almost legendary pictures like 'The Birth of a Nation', 'Broken Blossoms', 'Way Down East' and 'Orphans of the Storm', she was the fragile heroine, protecting her virtue against a hostile world. I was taken to see 'Orphans of the Storm' when I was about nine. At the climactic moment, when Miss Gish was being dragged to the guillotine, and it seemed the imminent rescue would arrive too late, the suspense apparently proved too much (clever Mr. Griffith!), and I turned to the adult I was with and said, "Don't worry, Auntie, it's only a picture!"

Lillian Gish now travels the world alone, showing Mr. Griffith's work with evident relish, and holding her audiences fascinated, as she explains the background to these early films in a delightful commentary, laced with humour — mostly against herself. The difficulty was to find a time in her diary when she could come to the BBC studios in Edinburgh, as I was anxious to do the interview, free from interruption, in the best accoustic surroundings. It was finally arranged for me to accompany her to a drama and poetry recital being given by her friend, Dame Sybil Thorndike, and then convey her to the BBC from there.

And so it turned out. We both greatly admired the superb artistry of Dame Sybil. My companion said she was humbled in admiration of anyone who could speak the English language with such beautiful cadences of voice. When we arrived at the BBC, we were met by one of the studio managers who seemed in a bit of a state. Apparently the studio I had booked was 'in a bit of a clutter' with props and sound effects for use in a radio play under rehearsal. Not perhaps, he thought, a tidy enough background for our distinguished guest. "Nonsense!" was her response, brushing aside all objections, "it's what I'm accustomed to . . . !"

A five-minute interview was what I had in mind, but, in the event, it stretched to nearly twenty minutes. I sent off the completed tape to the producer, for him to edit to his own liking. He not only used a five-minute version as asked for, he was so taken with the whole thing, that he gave it a separate programme on its own, under the title, 'The Silent Queen', and this went down so well that it has now been broadcast several times.

Let me tell you, if I may, about Tallulah's telegram. Not that I ever met Miss Bankhead. But on reading her autobiography some years ago, I was so impressed with the lady's wit and wisdom, that I sat down there and then, and wrote her a brief note in appreciation, simply addressing the envelope, 'Miss Tallulah

Bankhead, New York, U.S.A.' I did not get any immediate acknowledgement, nor did I expect any. And then, several months later, in my Christmas mail, I found a telegram from New York. This is what it said:—"Thank you so much, darling, Merry Christmas and a Happy New Year. Love, Tallulah".

I am often asked who is my favourite among the well-known people I have worked with over the years. This is a question to which I have never found the answer, because of course one likes different people for different qualities. But perhaps the person who made more of an impression on me than any other is Helen Keller. Her story is unique. She was a blind, deaf mute, who overcame her handicaps so successfully that it is fair to say there is no blind person to-day who does not owe something to Helen Keller, who devoted a long and full life to helping others. Not that she would ever take credit for this, insisting that it was all due to two things — her own deep, religious faith, and her 'beloved teacher'. The beloved teacher being Anne Sullivan Macey and the inspiring story has been made into a play and a film, called 'The Miracle Worker'.

When I met Helen Keller, she was an old lady and her companion, who had succeeded Anne Sullivan, was Miss Polly Thomson. Miss Thomson's brother was, for many years, Minister of Bothwell Parish Church, and Helen Keller was a frequent visitor at the Manse. The two ladies sat together on a settee, with me facing them, and I could see Miss Thomson's fingers moving deftly in Helen Keller's hand, as she transcribed what I was saying in terms of touch. My first impression of Helen Keller was of the tremendous amount of character in her face. It was a beautiful face, not because of the features, but because of the serenity in the expression. I canot find words to describe the quality of character that she conveyed. But I think, without even knowing her story, one would have felt in the presence of greatness. "So your name is 'Lockhart' ", she said, "are you descended from John Gibson Lockhart, who was Sir Walter Scott's son-in-law?" Her speech was thick and not easy to follow just at first, but I soon made her out. "Yes", I said, "at least we like to think so, although I understand he was not a very likeable man". "He may not have been likeable", she countered, "but if you're as clever as he was, you shouldn't complain!" Miss Thomson's fingers continued their work in Helen Keller's hand, as I went on, "Is there any message you can give me for our blind listeners?" I thought she had failed to comprehend, for she sat with head bowed. I looked at Miss Thomson, "Wait", she said, "Helen Keller never answers a question like that without thinking". I waited. Then she looked up. "Tell them", she said, "Tell them that sight comes from the soul; to have faith in God; and never, never to be sorry for themselves". When I asked her to amplify this a little, she went on, "Sight is not just a mere physical apprehending. When I was a girl and able to be taken for a walk by a sighted person, we might be greeted at home with the question, 'What did you see?' Nine times out of ten the sighted person would say 'Nothing much really . . .' This appalled me. Because I had seen things. For instance, I had seen the trees, because I could feel the leaves and the bark in my hands. I had seen the hay and the clover in the fields, I could smell them in my nostrils. But the sighted person was unaware of these things. You know", she continued, "there is the inner eye of understanding, which is often more highly developed in a blind person than in one who can see physically". I then said, "We're very proud to think that Miss Thomson, who's been with you all these years is a Scotswoman!" Again, there was no response, and then I realised Miss Thomson's fingers were still. "I couldn't tell her a thing like that", she said, "but you can if you like". "I don't understand", I said. "Just lean forward", she replied, and she lifted Helen Keller's hand and put it on my mouth and throat. "Now", she said, "just speak in your ordinary voice. You've got good diction". I repeated what I had said. Helen Keller smiled saying, "Oh I couldn't get very far without Polly", and then she added, "You can't get very far without the Scots!" This was not said for effect because she told me how she and Anne Sullivan used to spend holidays in the Scottish highlands, preferably by the sea. "I loved the salt sea breezes on my face, and the smell of the heather and the bracken in my nostrils".

I asked her if she felt she missed a lot in life. "I thank God every day for what has been granted to me", and then she went on, "But don't think I'm just a pious 'do-gooder'. I have my resentments too. I resent that I can never give Polly a present as a surprise. Either she or someone else has to know about it first, and it isn't the same. And I can never look into a shop window and choose for myself a smart hat or a dress. I have to depend on the choice of other people. But these are small things", she went on, "if it is God's purpose to use me in this way, I am content". These were the three words that lingered in my mind long after I had left her, **"I am content"**.

Then I got up to leave and went to the door with Miss Thomson. Then I turned and saw something different. I saw an old lady standing there with her head bowed, cut off, isolated, like a little island of loneliness. Something impelled me to go back. I touched her hand. And, as I did so, her face lit up like the switching on of a light. She shook my hand warmly, and thanked me for coming to see her. She thanked me! I can tell you, after I left her it was as if I was in some kind of trance. I must have walked for twenty minutes before my feet touched the ground, I was so elated by her wonderful personality.

My sister-in-law, Rita Stevenson Lockhart, once said to me, "You know, Howard, your only claim to fame is that your face has been touched by the hand of Helen Keller". And that is a distinction I am both proud and happy to accept.

CHAPTER 9

HOWARD'S FUN FAIR

I AM always chary of claiming to have made 'discoveries'. Most producers look back, with hindsight, and say with pride, "I discovered so-and-so". I am no exception, but I would hasten to add that those I am about to mention would undoubtedly have made their mark, without any initial assistance from me. All the same, there are some who have been kind enough to acknowledge my help in bringing them to the fore. They include Jimmy Shand, Margo Henderson, Ian Wallace, Kathie Kay, Frank Chacksfield and Alastair McHarg. I was also associated in their early days with Robert Urquhart, Michael Barratt, Cliff Hanley, Gordon Roddick, Peter Mallan, Ian Ross, Bryden Murdoch, the Five Smith Brothers and Moira Lamb.

As a gesture to me for giving him his first broadcast, Jimmy Shand much later wrote 'The Howard Lockhart Polka', which I now use every week in my Greetings Programme. Jameson Clark told me that, when it first came out, he was on tour with Jimmy and, half jokingly, said to him, "Here, Jimmy, I see you've written 'The Howard Lockhart Polka'. What about composing the Jameson Clark Waltz?" There was a pause, and then, with typical deadpan expression, the reply came quietly, "Aye, well I might. But you'll need to wait for eighteen years, as Howard did!"

Although generous in attributing her early broadcasting to me, Margo Henderson, like many another — myself included — graduated from Children's Hour and Kathleen Garscadden. Ian Wallace, on the other hand, was a complete amateur when I first heard him singing comic songs and playing the ukulele. I was instantaneously impressed, and accepted him immediately as suitable for Variety programmes. (He was then auditioned by the Music Department who, incidentally, turned him down!). At the time, I was producing a play called 'The Man With A Load of

Mischief' at the Park Theatre, and having difficulty in finding an actor for a leading male role. This was during the War, when few men were available. Ian impressed me by his voice, appearance and personality, and I decided to take a chance on him. Thus, Ian Wallace made his acting debut at the Park Theatre in Glasgow, and, from there, he has gone from one merited triumph to another.

Kathie Kay and Cliff Hanley were in a series of radio programmes I recorded from a cinema in Paisley. Kathie's husband, Archie McCulloch, was also involved. His contribution was to present newcomers to the microphone each week. Whether any of those selected were on their way to greater things, I now very much doubt. But there was one young man in the series who was certainly destined to become known. That was Cliff Hanley. In his colourful book, 'Dancing in the Streets', Cliff tells, in his own vivid style, how he initiated a series of 'cod' thrillers, featuring the unique adventures of one, 'Canny Reid, the Sauchiehall Street Sleuth'. There was nothing 'fishy' about them. They were pure surrealism, and in effect, they pre-gooned Goonery! I keep telling Cliff that Canny Reid was far too original an idea for oblivion.

During the War, a very shy, young man appeared for audition. He wore Army uniform as a full corporal, and was very quiet and diffident as he sat down at the piano, to sing songs of his own composition. His name was Frank Chacksfield. Last time I saw Frank, he told me he had kept the contract to remind him of his first broadcast.

Alistair McHarg sang from an aircraft factory in Prestwick in a series called, 'Works Wonders'. Gordon Roddick, now an announcer with STV, Ian Ross, now the BBC's Industrial Correspondent, and Peter Mallan, the singer, were all students in a class I ran, for a time, on Public Speaking. Robert Urquhart and I were in digs together after I came back from the Army. He had been invalided out of the Merchant Navy. He kept professing an interest in drama, especially acting, but I am afraid I

ON MY WAVELENGTH

didn't take him seriously. Then one day, John Stewart of the Park Theatre telephoned to ask if I knew of any young man who would be willing to 'walk on' in a production of 'The Queen's Husband'. Anyone would do, provided he was tall and could pass as a soldier. I immediately bethought me of Robert and he proved eager to accept. Within a week or so of rehearsals beginning, he came back to the digs one night, eyes dancing. "I've been promoted", he said, "I've been given a speaking part". In due course, I went to see the play. Robert was in the first act, and, I thought, quite dreadful! At the interval, John Stewart came over to me. "Thank you for sending us Robert Urquhart", he said, "we're all delighted with him!" Ah well, maybe I was wrong . . . ?

After the show that night, Robert wanted my opinion of his performance. "Do you want the truth?" I asked, "or shall I say how wonderful you were?" "I want to know **your** personal opinion", he replied. I told him. He wasn't exactly elated, but pestered me to tell him in detail what was wrong. In the end, I had to go over the part with him, line by line. He was insatiable for information and advice. I began to look at him in a different light. Here was someone who was anxious and keen to learn. I eventually gave him a part in 'Goodness How Sad' which was my next production for John Stewart. Robert's natural good looks were eminently suitable for the part of the film star. I was to follow this play with Barrie's 'Quality Street'. Robert knew this and kept asking me if he would get the part of Valentine Brown, the male lead. I told him no, this was a costume play and the part demanded experience and a style he had not yet had time to acquire. Shortly after, Robert went off on a brief visit to London "On business", he said. By the time he returned, I had given the part to another actor, and rehearsals were in progress. "A good thing you did for me, Howard, when you turned me down for Valentine Brown", said Robert. "I made up my mind there and then I was either going to put myself to the test, or give up this acting business altogether. I've been to London —

that was my business all right — but I sat an exam at the Royal Academy of Dramatic Art, and I've won the Korda Scholarship!" And so it happened that Robert Urquhart, whom I had turned down for Valentine Brown, was in a short time a successful West End actor, playing Horatio to Sir Alec Guinness's Hamlet, and taking leading parts in films.

The Park Theatre, under the amiable and shrewd direction of John Stewart, was a fruitful source of talent. Lea Ashton, son of Harry Ashton, for many years manager of the King's Theatre in Glasgow, served an apprenticeship at the Park and is now on the BBC staff. Bryden Murdoch appeared in three of my productions at the Park and went from there into radio plays. A very sensitive and responsive actor, Bryden has become a regular contributor to drama in radio, stage and television.

On the Variety side, I always welcomed 'Mr. and Mrs. Smith's Five Little Boys — the Five Smith Brothers' to the studio. Four of them were brothers. The fifth, though a Smith, was no relation. All five were my friends, and it was their habit every Christmas to send me a bottle of whisky. One year, there was a nasty scandal in BBC circles in London, when it was revealed that a member of staff had been taking expensive presents from dance band leaders, and bribery and corruption were being mentioned. Immediately, an edict was promulgated to the effect that no members of staff were on any account to accept gifts. One day, just before Christmas, the commissionaire phoned me and said, "Mr. Lockhart, the Smiths have just left a package for you. I think it's one you should come and collect in person". I could tell from his voice and manner that he knew what the 'package' contained. Down I went to collect it from the Reception Desk, just inside the front door, and, true enough, I could see from the size and shape that it was indeed a bottle. It was wrapped in a covering of thin brown paper. At the precise moment when I stretched out my hand to take it, the front door opened, and Mr. Dinwiddie, Controller for Scotland, came in. I saw him glance at the parcel, then at me, where he must have seen guilt written all over my face. "Brylcreem, Howard?" said he, and quickly walked past!

Michael Barratt, of 'Nationwide', was, when I first knew him, a young reporter on a Glasgow newspaper. More of Michael later. Moira Lamb, in her teens, took part in a production of 'Marigold' I did for a youth club in Anniesland. From there I took her to the Park Theatre for a small part in 'Pygmalion'. She did so well that John Stewart kept her in his company for a number of years. There she met his assistant, Kenneth Ireland, whom she married. And, from time to time, she appears in plays at the Pitlochry Theatre in the Hills, so ably run by her husband.

Even before I left the BBC to free-lance, I was able quite often to get permission to do outside stage work, which I still loved. The BBC's attitude swung between two extremes: Either 'by kind permission of the BBC' was to be absolutely obligatory on all programmes and in all publicity. Or, alternatively, on no account was the BBC to be mentioned at all. My first production for John Stewart at the Park was 'Pygmalion' in which the part of Eliza Doolittle was played by a most accomplished actress and broadcaster, Ann Downie, who gave it all up when she married a minister. Other productions I recall were 'Goodness How Sad' with Robert Urquhart and Moira Lamb; 'The Man With a Load of Mischief' with Ian Wallace, Bryden Murdoch, and that most elegant actress, Madeleine Christie; and 'Quality Street' with Marjorie Dalziel as a delightful Miss Phoebe. I greatly enjoyed working at the Park. Everything was so thoroughly professional and yet one was working in a small, homely atmosphere.

From the Park, I went to the New Victory Players, a group of hard-working and enthusiastic amateurs, who formed their club by way of celebrating the winning of the War. For them I did a number of productions and just before I left them, they allowed me to star in my own production of 'The Man Who Came to Dinner'. This was a piece of flagrant physical mis-casting, for the 'man' was supposed to be fat and gross, whereas I was tall and thin. However, I tried to make the most of my role of 'the world's rudest man' which no doubt came easily to me. We only changed one line in the play, and that, I submit, was an improvement. Where someone describes the 'man' as "that cannonball of fluff", I amended to "that streak of lean ham" — much more fitting for me, I assure you! Michael Barratt played the young reporter in the play (cast truly to type!) and he took part as juvenile lead in several of my New Victory productions.

I did a number of productions for various other clubs, although as a free lance I began to concentrate more on musicals which were so much more lucrative. Of these I particularly enjoyed 'The Quaker Girl' at Larbert and 'Lilac Time' at Dundee. I also look back with some pride and pleasure on the productions I did in the King's Theatre, Glasgow, of the 'Boys' Brigade Fanfare'. If not exactly 'with a cast of thousands', our numbers certainly ran into hundreds, credit for any success we achieved being shared among many officers and group leaders, not forgetting our musical directors, Bryden Thomson and Arthur Blake.

In radio, in addition to my record programmes, I contributed from time to time to 'Woman's Hour', and I was the regular presenter in Scotland of 'Home This Afternoon'. I was back in Children's Hour again too, in a series called 'Howard's Fun Fair'. Written by Lavinia Derwent, it purported to have me as a kind of genial uncle at a fairground. Fun to do and fun to be in. Not so funny, though, when, following an admonition from me to the children not to wander far away or "the wicked gipsies might steal you", we got a letter from some organisation representing the gipsies, threatening something approaching legal action, if we were so misguided as ever again to malign the fair name of the good gipsies!

Stewart Conn, poet and playwright, gave me the opportunity to adapt and read two of my favourite books as serials. One was

ON MY WAVELENGTH

'Annals of the Parish' by John Galt, the other was Stevenson's 'Travels With a Donkey'. Stewart is a particularly sensitive and sympathetic producer, and I recall these, especially the Stevenson readings as among the most satisfying things I have ever done on the air. My mother was a Stevenson, and she used to maintain that we were collateral descendents. Be that as it may, I know that, in working on his book, I found myself almost possessed by the author, so close are his ideas on philosophy and religion to my own.

I look back with rather more mixed feelings on my one and only appearance with the Scottish National Orchestra. Alexander Gibson invited me to be narrator in 'A Young Person's Guide to the Orchestra' and 'Peter and the Wolf' at concerts in the Usher Hall, Edinburgh, and St. Andrew's Hall, Glasgow. Edinburgh was fine. A packed house and an enthusiastic audience. In Glasgow, it was a very foggy night, and the hall was less than half full. Sam Bor, leader of the orchestra, had warned me that there was an extension to the platform that was inclined to wobble. He advised me to steady the score in front of me with my left hand. Thus forewarned, I clutched hard, and accidentally with my right hand, I turned two pages at once. I read the narration at the top of the page and realised my error at once. I panicked momentarily and Alec Gibson whispered to me out of the corner of his mouth to turn back and pick up the previous page. Fortunately, I could read music just well enough to pick up the right cue and away we went quite smoothly. But I felt I had let myself down badly that night. In self-defence I should add that people in the audience afterwards told me they had noticed nothing untoward. But the point was that I had noticed, Alec had noticed, and no doubt some of the orchestra had noticed. Afterwards, Alec dismissed the whole thing as of no consequence, but I must admit I was then grateful for the foggy night and the sparse attendance. Fortunately, the critics were most kind in their comments and ignored my lapse, which perhaps they did not notice.

HOWARD LOCKHART

Critics in general have been more than generous to me over the years, not only for my BBC programmes, but also as actor, producer and adjudicator. I was, however, for some time the target for some very harsh comments from one former critic of a Glasgow evening paper. To my knowledge I had never met the gentleman in question and it worried me that anyone should feel so vindictive about me, because his remarks went beyond the professional and were becoming more and more personal. After one particularly vicious attack, I entered the gates at Queen Margaret Drive feeling thoroughly despondent and depressed. Standing on the steps to greet me was the Reverend Ronald Falconer, Head of Religious Broadcasting in Scotland. "I am a Christian minister", he said, "and I try to put my Christianity into practice, but there is one radio critic I'd like to kick in the teeth!" I was worried for my parents and when the attacks were getting really serious, I spoke to my mother on the phone and told her I was thinking of taking action in some way. "Don't do any such thing", she counselled, "ignore it completely. Don't give him the satisfaction of knowing you've even read his comments". I followed her advice and, sure enough, his campaign of vilification petered out. Some time after, I met the critic and he admitted he had indulged in a deliberate vendetta against me, simply because of some imagined slight on my part. He further conceded that he had consulted the paper's lawyer to make sure his criticism was just on the legal side of libel.

For a few months, early in my career as a free lance, I myself enjoyed the role of radio critic with the Scotsman. At my interview, the editor said he would prefer me to remain anonymous and my weekly articles bore the credit, 'from our Radio Critic'. This suited me admirably as, although a free lance, I was still rather too close to the BBC personnel for my identity to be revealed. I hope I was able to maintain strict objectivity in my criticism, and I must admit I greatly enjoyed hearing people in the BBC discussing my comments, and then saying, "Who IS the

Scotsman critic these days, anyway?" The secret would doubtless have come out sooner or later, but, in the meantime, the BBC took me back on the staff to do temporary announcing, and I gave up my job as critic. But it was fun while it lasted.

As a free lance, I was able to accept much more work as an adjudicator of speech and drama. I had first adjudicated in drama before the War, at Inverurie and in Orkney. At Inverurie, I made a very nervous debut. At the interval, before they called me on to the stage, I ran into the well-known entertainer, Dufton Scott, who had worked in many of my radio programmes in Aberdeen. He was so kind and re-assuring that my self-confidence came flooding back.

In Kirkwall, I sat in the balcony, and the Chairman was in the stalls downstairs. He and I hadn't met. As I was collecting my notes, and making my way to the stage, I heard him introduce me in terms of extravagant praise I neither wanted nor warranted. He ended his introduction with the words ". . . And so, ladies and gentlemen, it is my pleasure to introduce Mr. Howard Marshall!" As I stepped on to the stage, I just had the presence of mind to say, that, while Mr. Marshall was a distinguished sports commentator, as far as I knew, the only thing we had in common was our Christian name!

Adjudicating seems to me to be a combination of experience, common sense and tact. I was often disastrously short in the last quality in my early days. Once in criticising a period play, I referred to one of the female characters and "that ill-fitting and unbecoming wig she wore!" Need I tell you how she greeted me afterwards? "Wig bedamned" she shrieked in aggrieved tones, tugging at her unruly mop, "That is my own hair!" On another regrettable occasion, I criticised one of the girls in a play for over-dressing the part. She appeared swathed in tartan and loud scarlet check, from tam o'shanter to scarf, blouse, skirt, stockings and brogues. "That", I said recklessly, "that is what I call 'Hoots, mon' Scots. It's what English calendars use as a caricature of the Scots!"

Her comment to me afterwards was direct and to the point. "That's what I wear every Sunday when I'm going to the Kirk!" To which I hastily replied, "And very becoming too, I'm sure (Lockhart, you liar!). But what is suitable in real life is not necessarily suitable on the stage". I was learning by this time . . .

The county of Argyll held a very special Drama Festival of its own, run by the enterprising Mr. R. Christie Park. Working for Bobby Park was always stimulating. His Festivals were social as well as artistic occasions. In fact, there were times when I used to find the social side just a little too much of a strain. At breakfast, Bobby would announce, "Well now, this morning we're having coffee with Mrs. So-and-so. Then we have lunch with Lord and Lady Such-and-such". (He was a great one for roping in the local gentry, was Bobby!). "After that, we'll be going for afternoon tea to call on . . ." And so it went on. All done with such easy charm, as one was whisked from one place to another often miles apart. I frequently wilted under the ceaseless barrage of social activity, wanting nothing so much as solitude to concentrate on the plays I was to judge in the evenings. But I needn't pretend I didn't also enjoy being lionised in this way, because I was secretly rather flattered. Just once, however, I was really angry with Mr. Park.

I was waiting patiently backstage one night for the stage to be cleared so that I might go on and give my adjudication after the last play. I always liked to do this with as little delay as possible. The audience is keyed up and ready to listen. It is bad psychology as well as bad manners to keep them waiting. This time the delay seemed rather long. "Aren't you ready yet?" I said to Bobby, rather testily as he emerged from the stage carrying some props. "It's all right", said he, as if to an impatient child, "don't panic!" With that he disappeared again on to the stage. Still I waited with growing indignation. Then, suddenly at the top of his voice, and audible to the entire audience, he shouted to one of his assistants, "Go and see if Mr. Lockhart's never ready yet!" I was furious. I stormed on to the stage ready to explode. Before I had time even to look round, the curtains swished open, and there I was, in full view of everybody. There was nothing for it but to stifle my rage and get on with the adjudication. And, of course, my anger quickly evaporated. By the time I came off, I could see the funny side.

Many of Bobby's most enjoyable Festivals were held in Ardrishaig, where I made many friends. He always made a great feature of his staging for the last night, with all kinds of beautiful flowers and plants from local estates. And one year, I had the privilege of making my entrance by walking down a white stair-case, exactly like the finale of a pantomime. Bobby Park was very much a showman, with a fine sense of theatre, and his Festivals always had an element of fun in them. Once, I am afraid, unintentionally. In the middle of one of the plays, the centre of the stage suddenly collapsed, and every light in the place went out. Substitute lighting was hastily improvised and the play resumed. Apparently the trestles, on which the stage was built, had somehow come adrift. The players, with immense resource, continued playing by moving gingerly round the edges of the hole visible in the centre of the stage. They continued as if nothing had happened, until the mother in the play had to make her entrance, saying, "Why is it that every time I leave this house, you'd think there was an earthquake!" At that, the house simply roared and then cheered its approval. In my adjudication after-wards I said, "I haven't consulted any of the officials for their consent, but I am nevertheless going to announce a special award to one team for its palpable triumph over adverse circumstances!"

At Bobby's Festivals, speeches on the last night were usually kept to a minimum. Unlike at some others, where audiences grew more and more restive under the sheer weight of boredom as one dreary speech followed another. Once the Chairman, at the end of an interminable list of people to get votes of thanks turned to me, and said calmly, "Now we come to the most impertinent man in the hall . . .'" A Freudian slip, perhaps?

HOWARD LOCKHART

I have adjudicated at festivals all over Scotland, in Northern Ireland and the North of England. Some of the most enjoyable are held in places like Preston, Nelson, Burnley, Morecambe and Lytham St. Annes. My most distant date was in Hong Kong, where they hold a splendid annual music Festival, including a large number of classes in speech and drama. I was appointed one year as adjudicator of the latter subjects and was thus enabled to embark on a second trip round the world. I began with some days in Bangkok, then some weeks in Hong Kong, and from there to Tokio, Honolulu and Hollywood. In Hong Kong, I was warned against making any kind of concession in marking the Chinese students, of whom there were vast numbers. They were eager to compete on exactly the same terms and standards as the Europeans and Americans. The caveat was hardly necessary, for I found so often that the Chinese spoke purer English than those whose native language it was.

I wonder how the myth of the 'impassive Oriental' came to be accepted. On the contrary, the Chinese have a positive love of drama and their features are most expressive. And their manners impeccable. Each competitor, on mounting the platform, would bow, first to me, then to the audience on one side of the hall, and then to the other. Before leaving the platform, the bowing order was reversed. And I noticed that when I announced the winners, the Chinese were the first to go over and shake hands with their successful competitors.

I found in the young Chinese a burning desire to speak English and to speak it well. Often they would follow me along the street, asking me just to talk to them. I found their eagerness most inspiring. I was invited to address the pupils of Queen Elizabeth College — founded by an Aberdonian incidentally — and when I got there, I discovered they had turned up to hear me, even although it was during the school holidays.

Once when I was in a lift at the hostel where I was staying in Kowloon, one of the amahs or servants looked at me, and noting the briefcase under my arm, said to me inquiringly, "You — teacher?" "No", I said, "no, I'm not really a teacher". She looked at me curiously again, saying, "What are you then — what do you do?" Just as I was trying to find a way of describing my function as an adjudicator, her face broke into a smile of comprehension, "I know", she said, "you are judge!" I nodded in agreement, and said, "Yes. In a way, you could say that". And, of course, she was right without knowing it. An adjudicator is an assessor, a judge — of quality and merit in a rather specialised field, but, none the less, a judge.

Another time, in a lull between classes, a Chinese girl, who was acting as steward, said to me, "Mr. Lockhart, are you British or American?" "Good gracious", I said, horrified, "can't you tell from the way I speak?" "Of course not", came the reply, "could you tell from their speech the difference between a Chinese and a Japanese? I know you are speaking the English language, but you might be of any nationality". I must say this gave me pause for thought.

Along with the music adjudicators — Sir Thomas Armstrong and Eric Thiman — I was interviewed on Radio Hong Kong. One of the producers asked me if I had ever heard of Lockhart Road. When I replied, "Of course. I have a contact there", eyebrows were raised. It turned out that Lockhart Road is the centre of Hong Kong's red light district. I hastily explained that my business was of another kind! I was interested in social service and had been told of a flourishing youth club in Lockhart Road. In due course, I found the youth club, which was run by a reverend father, and indeed he took me in his car along the full length of the street. The radio people suggested I might do a broadcast for them entitled, 'Lockhart on Lockhart Road, a symposium of sin, sex and social service'. I failed to comply.

I fell into a rather more orthodox assignment once in Monte Carlo. I was on holiday at Menton on the Riviera, when, by sheer co-incidence, I bumped into R. D. Smith, the London BBC producer. It transpired that he was on the lookout for good broadcasting material with which to compile a programme about the principality of Monaco. Before I knew it, I was roped in to help, and found myself running around Monte Carlo and the neighbourhood, giving my rusty French some much-needed polishing and practice in my search for suitable singers and entertainers.

Another year, I flew to Venice, and made recordings of various Scots I ran into there, as well as in Florence, Genoa and Paris. I was hot on the track of Scots accents and kilts! This was for a series I did from faraway places, called 'Lockhart's Log' (charmingly re-named in a Glasgow paper as 'Lockhart's Leg'!). A trip by ocean liner to the World's Fair in New York was the subject of another edition.

And then there was the time I was a guest at a Burns Supper in the Bahamas. I was staying in Nassau, with its lovely lagoons and beautiful beaches. It seemed decidedly odd to be eating tinned haggis and listening to records of Jimmy Shand, against a background of waving palms, the sea and the surf. I made some recordings of the proceedings with the assistance of a local radio engineer. Afterwards, he related how, as a hobby, he visited the island prison and helped the convicts to put on a show. It so happened that one was due in a few days' time. Would I like to go? I readily assented, and arrangements were duly made for my visit. On arrival, passing an armed guard, we were met by the prison Governor and taken into the hall where the concert was to be given. The place was packed with rows and rows of convicts, with armed policemen at the end of each row, and standing round the hall. The show proceeded with songs and comic turns, to which the audience responded noisily. Then came the fire dance. A large metal basin was set on the stage. It contained some highly inflammable fluid which was then lit, and a man began to dance in and out of the flames. It was all very exciting and the audience roared its approval. I sensed a slightly hysterical note in the reaction, and, down at the front where we were sitting, it was becoming decidedly warm. The dance came to an end and the dancer acknowledged the wild applause. Then he bent down and lifted the basin. But this had obviously not been rehearsed and he found it extremely hot. He lifted it in his bare hands, trying to pass it from one hand to the other, as he teetered off the stage. He had just got to the side when it became too much for him. He let go and dropped the basin. The audience shrieked as the flames took hold of the drapes at the edge of the stage. For a terrifying moment, it looked as if the whole place would go up in a blaze. And then, with great presence of mind, some of the prisoners rushed forward, grabbed the drapes in their bare hands, tore them down and stamped out the flames. The show then went on, without further mishap, but there was an air of suppressed excitement in the atmosphere, which I found disturbing. At the end of the performance, the Governor, to my dismay, invited me up to 'say a few words'. I hope I expressed my thanks adequately. I remember adding that, while I had heard of a show setting the place on fire, what we had seen was ridiculous!

CHAPTER 10

THE STORY OF MADELEINE SMITH

"YOU know, Howard, you'll need to learn to give of yourself!" Thus my mother to me in my student days, when she heard me on the phone haggling over whether or not there was a fee attached to some public appearance I was asked to make. I don't suppose I paid much attention at the time, but since then I have often remembered her admonition and appreciated its value. I consider I have been singularly fortunate in having been able to do so many of the things I wanted to do, and in getting paid for doing them. So I like to redress the balance a bit, and give my services to various worthy causes, without getting material reward. My mother was right. Without, I hope, sounding priggish, the satisfaction comes from the giving of oneself.

The Reverend J. Stanley Pritchard has, from time to time, provided me with opportunities to help various organisations through his radio and TV appeals in the series, 'The Week's Good Cause'. Stanley, over the years, has proved a tremendous public benefactor in arranging so many Appeals, ably assisted by his secretaries, Helen Paterson and Barbara Fergus. (Incidentally, Helen Paterson was formerly my secretary when I was on the BBC staff, and she and her successor, Nancy Robertson, share equally in the credit for anything I was able to achieve in those days). I have been delighted, through these Appeals, to collect funds for a number of worthwhile organisations. If I mention only two of them — namely, LEPRA, the Leprosy Relief Association, and the Benevolent Fund for Nurses — it is because I have worked more often on their behalf.

On one occasion, Barbara Mullen and I made a joint TV appeal in London for the Nurses' Fund, a Cause that is near to our hearts. Soon after that, Barbara came to Glasgow for an extended period during the run of 'Dr. Finlay's Casebook'. Like Andrew Cruickshank and Bill Simpson, she proved friendly and approachable. I very much wanted her to record an interview with me for the magazine programme, 'Home This Afternoon', but it proved difficult to fit this in with her heavy programme of rehearsals for 'Dr. Finlay'. However, at last it was fixed that she would meet me at the Reception Desk at Queen Margaret Drive, immediately after her rehearsal one afternoon. In the early stages of rehearsing, the Finlay cast worked in a hall some distance from the studios, so I volunteered to collect her by taxi. No, this wouldn't do at all, she said, she didn't know the exact moment when she would be free. Sometimes the producer kept them late. All the more reason, I ventured, for my being there to whisk her to the studio. But that, according to Miss Mullen, wouldn't do at all; No; she would come on her own. She wouldn't be late, she assured me. I was not reassured at all, because, if her rehearsals ran late, my recording arrangements would break down. So, on the day, I made for the studio fully half an hour early, just to be sure everything would be in complete readiness for her arrival, late though it might be . . . It was a waste of worry on my part. When I arrived at the Reception Desk on my way in, there was the lady, calmly waiting. Seeing incredulity written all over my face, she gave me a real Janet-of-Tannochbrae look and said, with a twinkle, "Life is full of surprises, Howard!"

After making an Appeal, there was always a certain anticipation and excitement in watching the result as the donations rolled in, and the total increased. But, in my experience, there has been no heady excitement to surpass that of opening night of one's own stage play.

I was producer for the New Victory Players when I first got the idea to write a play about Madeleine Smith, the Glasgow girl of good family who was accused of murdering her illicit lover. That is not quite true perhaps, for the idea had lain dormant for years. My father, a lawyer, had volumes of the Notable Scottish

Trials in our house, and he liked to tell visitors about the fascination of the Trial and, in particular, of her defence. His interest was in the legal aspect. Mine was different. I was always intrigued by the domestic side. The idea of this bold, unconventional young lady, living a life of deception, entertaining her lover secretly in her own home against a background of such solid respectability — all this I found compelling and full of dramatic possibilities.

At a meeting of the New Victory Players, members said they thought a large part of the success they had won, was due to choosing plays well out of the ordinary rut. Would I suggest another? Without really thinking, I pointed out that the best way to get a play out of the rut, was to write one. "There's Michael there", I said, pointing to Michael Barratt, at that time a young reporter on a Glasgow newspaper, "why not get Michael to write a play for you?" Quickly he returned the ball into my court, "Will you write one with me then?" I liked Michael, and I liked the New Victory Players, so I said yes! And that is how the whole thing got started. Michael and I arranged to get together and discuss some ideas. We parted, and, in the meantime, I thought of Madeleine Smith again. At our next encounter, we discussed the possibilities. Michael liked the idea, but knew little of the case. At that time, I was living in a flat in Sauchiehall Street, just round the corner from the Smith's former home in Blythswood Square, where it all took place. We walked round the building, while I described the course of events. He and I were about to part for the summer holidays, and we agreed that we'd each try to write down some ideas, as a basis for a play, and discuss them together on our return.

At this time I was still with the BBC, and used to spend part of my holiday in Blackpool, looking for acts for broadcasting. This turned out to be a very wet holiday, and I decided I might as well start on the play. I wrote and wrote, my only source of reference being the book of the Trial, which includes in an appendix, most of the letters Madeleine wrote to her lover, in other words, the letters she was at such pains to recover. I immersed myself in these outpourings of a troubled spirit, and, in fact, much of the dialogue in the play consists of Madeleine's own words. The more I wrote, the more fascinated I became. In later years, I was to find that some people affect to despise the play because it is based on the Trial, and not entirely an original creation. I submit that it is easier to invent complete fiction, than to adapt from documented fact, which imposes severe limitations of truth.

When Michael and I met again, it turned out that he had not had the opportunity to write anything. So I invited him to my flat, along with another friend, to hear what I had got down. I had, in fact, completed a draft of the play. As I read it out that night, insisting on sitting with my back to the others while I did so, I became aware by the very atmosphere that the play was going down well. I take no credit for that, because the subject of Madeleine Smith has an eternal fascination of its own. But when I had finished, they were both obviously impressed favourably. So I was then invited to read it to the Club. I impressed upon them beforehand that they would do me a dis-service if they praised the play without really approving of it. It was up to them. Again, there was this extraordinary response. Yes, they very much wanted to do the play.

Rehearsals began. Instead of the usual small-talk afterwards, people broke into little groups discussing the Non-proven verdict which acquitted her of the crime, and the inevitable question, did she do it or didn't she? The show was booked for three or four nights in the Glasgow Lyric Theatre. I was anxious that the Smith drawing room would look authentic and reflect the taste and style of its Victorian inhabitants. I impressed on the scene-hirers that I must have a double door leading into the room — a double door was essential. And I got it all right. Oh yes, it was a double door, but imagine my feelings on arrival at the dress-rehearsal to find the double door was the upper halves to the slatted swing-doors leading into an American western saloon! Fortunately, there was time to have it changed for the opening the next night.

On the first night, I slipped into the back of the circle to try to sense the mood of the audience. Yes, they did seem to be completely absorbed. The response at the end was enthusiastic. Now what would the papers say? That was the next thing. Talk about excitement, as I sat up waiting for the reports . . . all of which were good, some rather grudging, it is true, but none unfair or unkind. I was particularly elated by the comments of the critic of the Glasgow Herald, Colin Milne, whose words I always respected. Of my play he said, "In every way this is a good play, well-knit, credible, with no loose threads . . ." Although I have, since then, seen many performances of my play, by professionals as well as amateurs, I still regard the New Victory Players' production as, in a way, the definitive one (in which, incidentally, Michael Barratt played the part of Madeleine's brother, Jack). When I visualise the characters in my mind's eye, I see them as they appeared in that original presentation. Some time after, I was approached by the Glasgow Citizens' Theatre to send them a copy of the play, and, in due course, they decided to put it on. Word came back to me that James Bridie had liked it. The producer was to be John Casson, and he came to see me to discuss various points, including the question of casting. Madeleine was to be played by Anna Burden, an actress of great dramatic intensity. Bryden Murdoch was to be her lover, and others in a fine cast, included Peter Macdonell, Lennox Milne, Laurence Hardy, Pearl Colquhoun, Ethel Glendinning and Gudrun Ure.

I deliberately kept away from rehearsals, knowing as a producer, how awkward it is to work with the author breathing down your neck. But apparently I overdid the detachment, for John Casson phoned and told me it was being whispered that I wasn't interested. I immediately put in an appearance. It was a strange experience. There was my play, with my words, being walked out by players in their ordinary clothes in the grim pilot light of an empty theatre. I sat quietly, waiting and watching. I realised that here was a different production from mine in so many ways, but it was compelling, none the less. When the rehearsal was over, I was invited up to the stage to comment. I thanked the cast and made some minor suggestions. To start and re-produce the play was not my intention. I could be detached enough to recognise virtue in another interpretation and I was quite satisfied to leave it at that.

Monday, 27th September, 1948, was opening night. Perhaps the most exciting experience of my life. I had been told to wear a dinner jacket and I knew I might have to make a curtain speech. Sir Lewis Casson and Dame Sybil Thorndike, John Casson's parents, were to be present, as well as James Bridie, Ivor Brown, drama critic of the Observer, A. J. Cummings of the News Chronicle, and many other distinguished critics. "I've got a seat for you with my father and mother", said John Casson, when I arrived at the Citizens' that night. "OH NO!" I said, "I couldn't possibly sit still, far less in such company. Thank you, John, but no!" "Where are you going to sit then?" he asked, "the theatre's full". "I'm going as far out of sight as possible", I said, "I'll stand at the back of the circle". And I did. He joined me there and by the end of the first act, it was pretty clear that all was going well. The moment the curtain fell, I ran straight to John's office and shut myself away from the crowd. I was just in process of going through some of the telegrams of good wishes, when the door opened and James Bridie walked in. Although I knew him well and had worked with him at BBC, we had not met during the preliminaries of my play. He was very short-sighted and didn't see me at first. As soon as I spoke to him, he came forward and shook my hand, "Oh, it's you, Lockhart", he said, "congratulations!" "Thank you", I replied, "but you've only seen the first act". "Ah yes", he said, "but don't forget I've read the play". His subsequent comment in a letter to me was, "This is a play that can hold up its head in any company of good plays". He also

113

commended it for practical reasons. "It is always a good thing to write a play with a good part for a leading actress, because then you will find actresses who want to do it!"

By the fall of the final curtain, there was no doubt of the play's success. "Follow me", said John Casson, and blindly I went with him along a narrow corridor and down a steep stair. Then I panicked. I heard the applause, I saw John step on to the stage under the lights, and I panicked. I started to run. I made for the stage door. I was nearly there when I was stopped by Penny Skelton, the stage manager. "Come on, Howard", she said, catching hold of me by the sleeve, "they're calling for you!" Gently she led me back and gave me a warm smile of reassurance as I stepped on to the stage. My nerves were gone now. I made my few remarks, and as the curtain fell, shutting out the audience, I turned and kissed Anna and thanked everybody for the success they had made of my play.

Later I met the celebrities in the audience, including Sir Lewis and Dame Sybil. They were naturally enthusiastic about their son's production, but they were very, very kind in their remarks to me about the play. I saw quite a lot of them subsequently, for they were appearing in Priestley's play, 'The Linden Tree' which followed mine at the Citizens'. (The play preceding mine had been 'Dear Brutus', and I must admit to considerable pride at being bracketed between Barrie and Priestley!). Once I made some mild criticism because a line or two of the dialogue had been revised. "Don't worry about that", advised Dame Sybil, "shall I tell you something? There are quite a few lines in the published edition of 'Saint Joan' that are not by George Bernard Shaw — they're pure Sybil Thorndike", she said, with her characteristic chuckle. "Of course", she added hastily "of course, I asked Mr. Shaw if I could change a line here and there, and he used to say, 'My dear, if you feel it's better that way, then do it that way!' "

The following year I went to Australia, taking a copy of my play, which had been published in the meantime. In Sydney I produced it, both on the radio and the stage. The Australians loved it and, not knowing about the factual background, gave me credit for invention. One lady wrote and said she thought I had been so subtle in naming the two Smith sisters, 'Madeleine' for the glamorous, unconventional heroine, and 'Bessie' for the demure young Victorian miss!

After my return to Scotland, the play was broadcast by the BBC and then, later, it was televised by Rediffusion in their studios at Wembley. I was in London at the time, doing 'Housewives' Choice', so I could go to rehearsals and watch the play developing in another medium. Robert Urquhart brought his experience of television to bear on the adaptation and Zena Walker and John Phillips brought distinction to the parts of Madeleine and her autocratic father.

I have since seen many productions of my play and I must admit I always enjoy them! I particularly recall productions in Perth, with Nora Laidlaw and David Steuart. Gordon Jackson played the brother, the part originally done by Michael Barratt. And, one of the most satisfying productions of all, at the Pitlochry season. Madeleine was played by Moira Lamb, and the cast also included Victor Carin and Una McLean. Una was cast in the unlikely part of Madeleine's mother!

People often ask me why I haven't written other plays. The answer is — I have! But none of them have been successful. 'Consequences' which is now in published form, has been done once or twice by amateurs, following my initial production of it for the New Victory Players. I am very fond of it, for there is much of me in it, but I readily realise it has its shortcomings. It opens at a silver wedding, flashes forward in the second act to a golden wedding, then, in act three, reverts to the silver wedding. The twenty-five year gap, forward then backward, does present problems of make-up to the players.

'The Story of Madeleine Smith' has had productions every year somewhere during the last twenty-five years. And there is life in

115

the enigmatic lady yet. The TV people made me change the title to 'House of Lies', the original title not being they said, 'dynamic enough'! At Pitlochry, to suit the billing, it was called just 'Madeleine Smith'. I think perhaps this is an improvement. I decided originally on the longer title, simply because I wanted the play to be regarded as a story founded on fact, rather than as a factual reconstruction of events.

When people ask me, as they invariably do, if I think Madeleine was guilty, I always say I don't know. I think there are good reasons for believing her innocent of the crime of which she was charged. She could have done it, she says in the play, and that is as far as I am prepared to go. Except to add that, as she was twenty-one at the time of the Trial and lived to be over ninety, I think it highly unlikely that any woman could keep a secret so well hidden for so long!

CHAPTER 11

ON THE TELLY

"WHY don't we see you more often on the telly, Howard?" they say. Or, "You never get on TV, do you, Howard? You're only on the radio". I don't much care for the word 'only', but of course, the implication is true. My reputation, such as it may be, has been built through my voice. Which is maybe just as well. I cannot pretend to be enthusiastic about my appearances on television. No one else has shown much enthusiasm either. And yet, surprisingly, I have done quite a variety of TV jobs over the years. I have, at various times, been an actor, interviewer, interviewee, panellist and playwright.

I must say I enjoyed the playwright bit! It gave me a great thrill to attend rehearsals and watch the final shooting of 'House of Lies', adapted for the new medium by Robert Urquhart, from my stage play 'The Story of Madeleine Smith'. Perhaps not quite as exciting as preparing for a first night in the theatre, but undeniably stimulating to see the various elements coalesce, from the preliminary reading, right through to the actual performance for the screen. And I have to admit I rather enjoyed playing the role of author. Especially when I first presented myself for admission to rehearsal at Rediffusion's studios at Wembley. "Name, please?" says the commissionaire at the reception desk, consulting a typed list in front of him. I tell him. "I don't see any Lockhart", he says. "That's funny, it should be there", I say, deliberately casual. "Are you in the cast?" he asks. "No, but the producer knows I'm coming", I say, blandly. "I'll ring him and ask him", he says, reaching for the phone. And then I tell him, "I'm the author", I say, and may heaven forgive me for making such a meal of it!

And then, I 'sit in' with the producer, his secretary, the vision mixer, the sound mixer and various other people of technical skill whose job it is to make a composite whole out of the various separate contributing parts. We face a row of television screens, each one relating to one camera, and I try to remember to concentrate on the 'master' set, which is showing the finished product as it will go on the air. But I must admit to being fascinated by some of the others, where one can see the players when they are **not** acting, but just waiting to do their scene. Some of them fidget, adjusting their unaccustomed clothing. Others look keyed up in anticipation. Others again appear to look quite casual. I wonder if they are nervous at all. They certainly don't look it. I don't suppose I did either, when I was waiting for a cue, but the strain was always there, none the less.

My first TV appearance was in Moultrie Kelsall's play, 'Who Fought Alone', produced by James Crampsey, with Frank Wylie as the wretched soldier fighting against the enemy and his own destiny. I was a particularly unsympathetic 'burroo' clerk, to whom poor Frank applied in vain for help. I had to sit in a tiny little space, behind a netted grille, and there I was seen doling out allowances to various unemployed men in front of Frank in the queue. The unemployed were played by students from the College of Drama. Until Frank appeared at my window, all I had to say was "Next, please" as monotonously as possible. At first I was given real money to dish out, but apparently this did not photograph well. So we then tried chocolate money wrapped in gold paper, the kind that children love. This was fine, they said. Fine, at rehearsals, yes. But, with the heat from the lights, the chocolate began to melt, and soon I was handing over great gobs of sticky brown mush to the unfortunate 'extras', who had then to pocket it!

Next, I was in a couple of period plays adapted from novels. Both had as titles, the names of their respective heroines, 'Mary Barton' and 'Esther Waters'. In 'Mary Barton', I was Clerk of the Court in a trial scene. This suited me admirably, because all I had to do was to administer the oath to the witnesses. But something happened in 'Mary Barton' which was to affect me more than I realised at the time. Our scene had been thoroughly rehearsed, over and over again, by the time we came to the recording of the whole play. But, on the actual 'take', in the middle of our scene, one of the principals 'dried' — he forgot his lines. There was a terrible pause as we waited in uneasy silence. Then the ice-cold voice of the producer came through the loudspeaker, "Cut! We'll have to go back". What made it all the more embarrassing was that this should happen now, in front of all the 'extras' who had been brought in as jurors and spectators. After a long wait, while it was decided where we should pick it up again, the rehearsal was resumed. And did the same actor not dry up again, at exactly the same bit! Again, it was a case of "Cut! We'll go back" as the actor, under great strain, tried to apologise. Everyone was sympathetic, knowing how he felt. The third time, all went well.

I love the illusion created in a studio by sheer make-believe. In 'Mary Barton' there was one particular scene that fascinated me. On the TV screen, as it was shown, one saw the heroine handling the oars in a rowing boat, as she bravely battled her way across the water. In actual fact, she was sitting in a cut-away of half a rowing boat, and she had been lifted and put there by a floor-manager wearing Wellington boots, so that her feet and ankles would not get wet. The cut-away of the boat was in fact sitting on the studio floor in three inches of dark, dirty water. On the screen, with the wind machine blowing her hair back, and the cry of the seagulls, you could have sworn she was in the open sea!

In 'Esther Waters' I had a bigger part. I was a rather forbidding, Victorian solicitor, with one good scene, in which I was to convey to the lady of the manor the disturbing news that her profligate husband had dissipated the family fortune. While we are talking, a shot is heard. She looks at me, saying "Where did you leave my husband?" To which I gave the significant reply, "In the gun-room!" When the script arrived, it gave no details about the rest of the cast, so I went to the first rehearsal wondering with whom

I was to play the scene. On arrival at the dark, rather damp church hall where we rehearsed (if anyone thinks being in TV is full of glamour, let them just try a few rehearsals), I was delighted to find I was playing opposite Pauline Letts, a splendid actress whom I had last seen on the London stage, with Robert Morley in 'Edward My Son'. She and I hit it off at once and, largely thanks to her, I enjoyed the scene and played it with confidence.

The producer gave me a wonderful entrance through a double door, my arrival being announced by a maid, in full uniform. I was dressed in the dark morning-clothes of the period, and I carried a brief-case under my arm. The camera followed me through the door, so that only my back was seen. In my sombre clothes I did indeed look like the harbinger of doom. What I did not realise, while I was doing the scene, was that the camera was focussed on my hands holding legal documents, so that the viewers were spared — mercifully? — the sight of my face.

There was some slight trouble with the off-stage shot, I remember. The first time it went off, it nearly lifted Pauline from her chair. In fact, we both nearly hit the roof, it was so loud. Next time, it was so quiet we didn't hear it at all and made a hash of our cues. However, it was repeated again and again, until the producer was satisfied. And then we embarked on the actual 'take'. "Where did you leave my husband?" said Pauline, after the fatal shot. Just as I was about to give her the dramatic answer, the unmistakable noise of a jet overhead assailed our ears. "Cut!" called the producer, cursing the anachronism, and that was another scene ruined. Back I went through the double door, and, when all was quiet, we did it again. As shown on the screen, the camera very rightly lingered on Pauline's expressive face for her reaction to my doom-laden line, so, all in all, what with my hands in the early part of the scene, and her face later on, the viewers were spared the over-exposure of the Lockhart countenance.

Next, I was a member of the French Academy in 'The Scarlet and Black'. John Stride had the leading role, and I had one good scene with him, in which I had to speak some Latin. Whether it was this extra burden or the 'Mary Barton' episode, or, more likely, a combination of both, I do not know, but more and more I was aware of strain in memorising lines. Eventually, for health reasons, I was forced to give up the part. Rather ironical, then, that the actor who took over from me was provided with 'idiot boards' for the Latin. (Idiot boards are little blackboards, held just out of camera range, from which the actor can read). I had learned my lesson. I realised that, although I had never 'dried' on my lines, I was always terrified that I might. And, further, I found the inevitable hanging around at rehearsals very tedious. Other actors would be playing Scrabble or doing crosswords, while the actresses were interminably knitting. Me, I was just plain bored. So, from then on, I refused all acting jobs and gradually offers ceased. I cannot honestly say that TV drama has suffered irreparably in consequence. Pity . . .

Twice I have been interviewed on the telly. Once by Mary Marquis, a lady with a beautiful voice, who always sounds as attractive as she looks. And once, by Larry Marshall in the famous "One O'clock Gang", an experience which I thoroughly enjoyed, thanks to the friendliness of everybody at STV. Likewise, I have twice done the interviewing. Once with the delightful Scots actress, Sophie Stewart, and once with that splendid and, in my view, neglected player, Jean Kent. To conclude the sum total of my vast TV experience, I was in 'Sense and Nonsense', with Magnus Magnusson in the chair; I have made two Appeals, one with Barbara Mullen for the Nurses, and one on behalf of the Glasgow Old People's Welfare Committee; and I once read the lesson in a Church service.

To say I did not care for myself at all on the small screen is a supreme understatement. I thought I was terrible. Most people who see themselves possibly react in the same way. A well-known writer tells me she runs and hides behind the door, listening to her voice, but unable to look at herself. For myself, I have never really felt relaxed or confident under the eye of the camera. There are those who say this would come with experience. Possibly. But I have now neither the patience nor the inclination to persevere. On the other hand, I normally feel completely at ease and at home in radio, where I can remain unseen and unseeing. But then of course I grew up with broadcasting. I love every aspect of it. Perhaps especially the kind of greetings programme I present, where I try to establish an immediate contact with listeners, imagining I hear their reply when I ask, "How are you to-day?"

When one appears on television after being known only by sound, illusions can be shattered. After seeing my tall, lean figure on the small screen, a regular listener wrote, ". . . it gave us such a surprise, because, from your voice, you sound like a fat, bald-headed, old man!" Once, following an afternoon talk I had given to an audience of old people, on arrival at the station for the return journey to Glasgow by train, I found the platform deserted. But there was a little bookstall, so I asked the girl behind the counter when the next train was due. "Oh", she said, "you've just missed one. You'll need to wait for half an hour". Well, we had a little chat, then I went for a short walk to fill in the time. When I returned to the station and went forward to the bookstall to buy an evening paper, I noticed the girl's face was wreathed in smiles. "It's funny", she said, "but when you were talking to me just now, I could have sworn I recognised your voice". "Oh yes?" I said, rather expectantly. "Oh yes", she went on, "you sound exactly like that Howard Lockhart that speaks on the wireless". "Do you really think so?" I asked. "Oh you're the dead spit!" she replied. Still the penny had not dropped. So, prompting her, I looked her straight in the eye and said, "Well, I have been told that before". "Oh," she ploughed on, "I'm not surprised. Mind you, he's a bit more polished than you are!"

In a burst of confidence, another regular listener wrote, "It's not everyone I take a fancy to, dear Howard. I'm in my forties now, but still hoping . . ."

122

CHAPTER 12
HOW ARE YOU TO-DAY?

F OR many years, the presentation of 'Housewives' Choice' was considered the plum job in record programmes.. It was a network programme from London, as opposed to my own weekly broadcast, which is confined to Scotland. Accordingly, I decided to aim at the larger audience, and a tape of my own show was sent to Anna Instone, head of gramophone programmes. Back came word that I had been accepted for 'Housewives', and, in due course, a contract arrived and off I went to London, on the first of many annual visits.

Wouldn't you just know it, the very first morning, I went to the wrong studio! I had to report for rehearsal at seven-fifty at Broadcasting House, so I was up, bright and early, with a taxi ordered to get me there by a quarter to eight. Nothing like being in good time, and creating a good impression, I thought. But alas! I must have mistaken the number of the studio. I was on the right floor, but I must have taken the wrong turning. Oh I was in a studio right enough, sitting there waiting for what seemed like ages, but no one appeared. I put this down to London sophistication. But when it came to ten past eight, "To hell with this", I thought, "there's such a thing as being too casual!" And off I went on a voyage of exploration. Back down to the Reception Desk to check. And there I found the producer in a panic, wondering what had happened to me! By this time, I was a bit panicky myself, but I thought "No! this is my first morning. I refuse to let anything upset me". And I didn't. Fortunately, all went well thereafter, and my name was added to the select rota of those annually allocated a spell on the programme.

The length of one's term of office varied from one to three weeks. No one was ever allowed on the programme more than once a year. This was to ensure that the show was always more

HOWARD LOCKHART

important than the presenter, and, of course, to introduce a variety
of styles. When it was my turn, I used to go through the post
cards and build programmes. It was never a case of just picking
up a bundle of cards at random and working haphazardly. No, it
took a long time, sifting through the requests and building
balanced programmes. I used to spend enjoyable days in the
gramophone library, just playing over different records, deciding
if they were suitable or not.

During the weeks I was on the air, I was up at six every
morning, and off to the studio by taxi from my hotel in Knights-
bridge. I used to love these early morning trips through Hyde
Park, often when it was still dark. When the broadcast was over,
I went to a cafe near the BBC for breakfast. There I was often
joined by friends who knew they would always find me there.
Anne Shelton came from time to time, and so did Donald Peers,
George Elrick and David Hughes.

One year, we had a break in each programme for a Food Flash.
These were given by my Glasgow chum, Molly Weir, or Ruth
Drew, the cookery expert. I had often admired the latter's lovely
voice, and pictured her as tall and willowy. To my surprise, she
was plump and round, with a jolly, beaming face. She used to
arrive at the studio panting, having cycled through Hyde Park.
She was a very delightful person, with a superb broadcasting style.

From time to time, there were ugly rumours of bribery, and what
is unattractively designated as 'payola', in connection with the
programme. A popular programme, with such a huge audience
was obviously a target for the publishing and recording companies,
as a shop window for their wares. All I can say is, I was virtually
shadowed by the pluggers, but never once was I offered anything
in the nature of a bribe. Certainly they would ask me out to
lunch, but never more than once during each visit. Sometimes I
accepted, being always careful to add, "But of course, you do
realise that I can't do anything for you, since it is a request programme". It was not unknown of course for some of the less

scrupulous pluggers to write in requesting their own records. But I soon found the producers for whom I worked could sniff out a phoney card on sight. I remember once going into a producer's office, and finding him sitting with his feet up on the desk, as he sifted through a bundle of cards and threw them, one by one, into the waste-paper basket across the room. "They're all phoneys" he said, "every stricken one of them!" When I asked how he could tell, "When you've been doing this for as long as I have", he said, "you develop a scent for the bogus!"

Once, after a programme, one of the record pluggers thanked me profusely because I had included one of his records in the broadcast that morning. "Oh, was that yours?" I said, "I didn't know". His mouth dropped open in amazement and incredulity. He didn't know whether to believe me or to be indignant with me. But I **didn't** know . . . I used to get the feeling that I was regarded as something of a country cousin, innocent and incorruptible. I tried to preserve that illusion.

There was a good deal of rivalry among the disc-jockeys in London, but those that I met were always extremely friendly and kind, especially David Jacobs, Pete Murray and Sam Costa. Twice when I was in London, my visits coincided with the Radio Show at Earls Court, and twice I did programmes from Radiolympia. I must admit I was very thrilled to see my photo, along with those of other disc-jockeys, on the front cover of Radio Times. But, wouldn't you know it? in Scotland they had different covers on both occasions.

One day I was having lunch with Benny Lee in a restaurant much patronised by show people, when a lady rose from a nearby table and came across to us. "I just wanted to say how much I am enjoying your presentation of 'Housewives' ", she said to me, "because you always manage to sound so sincere". Slightly overcome by the source of this compliment, I stammered my thanks no doubt inadequately. But, coming from her, I valued the tribute and knew it to be genuine. It was Vera Lynn.

HOWARD LOCKHART

Going through the cards of requests, trying to decipher writing often difficult to read, and then deciding which most merited inclusion — it all took a lot of time and preparation. I had, in fact, very little opportunity for social life. Sometimes the cards would turn up little gems of misapprehension. "A song from Arabella Fonti" obviously meant a record of Harry Belafonte. But I was much puzzled by a request for the song, 'Good Boy'. I searched in vain through the comprehensive indices in the BBC's marvellous gramophone library, trying always to resist being side-tracked by other alluring titles I met on the way. In the end, I took my problem to one of the clerks. He looked at the card, and at once his face lit up with a smile. "Easy", he said, "what they want is not 'Good Boy', it's 'Goodbye'! You go by the sound, not the spelling". When I later lifted a card asking for the "Scotch song about Our Young Canary", I merely had to rephrase vocally for me to realise it meant, 'I'm Ower Young To Mairry'! And we all chuckled at the idea suggested on the card with the request for Andy Stewart singing, 'The Chocolate Soldier'!

Apart from the requests, there was always a fair amount of fan mail to be read and, of course, acknowledged. One lady wrote and said, "I think you may be interested to know, that while you were doing 'Housewives' Choice' the other morning, my daughter gave birth to a bouncing baby boy!" I frankly failed to see what this arrival had to do with me. But she went on, "And she and her husband have decided to call him Howard, after you!" Another wrote, noting my habit of pausing for a reply when I gave my morning greeting, "What a thrill I get when I hear you say 'good morning, how are you?' I just push my head closer to the wireless by my bedside, and I say, 'Good morning, darling, how are you?' ! "

I invariably enjoyed my annual trips to London for 'Housewives' Choice', but I was always glad to be home again, doing my own programme in my own way. There were times, I admit it, when I was tempted to settle in London and make my home there. I even went as far as examining the prospects for regular radio work, and found these distinctly promising. But the London life is hard and hectic and I was not convinced I could stand the pace, even with all its manifold attractions. Also, I was unwilling to give up the work I so much enjoyed in Scotland where I had my roots — the lecturing, the adjudicating, and, most compelling of all — my own radio programme which, by this time, I had come to regard as something of a mission.

It had come to me, following my long spell in hospital near Aberdeen. As a patient, I had been very touched when my old friend, Sandy MacPherson, sent me a greeting in his programme. I had never realised until that moment, just what it can mean to have a radio greeting in this way, when you are ill and in hospital. What impressed me particularly, and much to my surprise, was the tonic effect it had on the entire establishment. Everyone was talking about 'our' hospital having been mentioned over the air. Even nurses who had been off duty came tearing along the corridors, saying, "What's all this about our hospital having been mentioned on the radio?" A further greeting was broadcast to me later, in the 'Housewives' Choice' programme, and, once again, there was this tremendous upsurge of interest. I lay in bed thinking about it. Here, I thought, was something I could do. Maybe the very fact of having been a long-term patient would help to give me an understanding of the special needs of those in hospital, or otherwise 'shut-in'. And thus I planned my course of action, if I were ever in a position to provide a programme for those to whom, it seems to me, the need is greatest.

And thus it was that, on my return to health and the BBC, I managed to persuade the planners to let me try out a programme of greetings, where I could pack in as many names as possible with each record. In hospital, I had noticed it was the mentioning of names, not the music that mattered. It used to vex me in 'Housewives' Choice' and other programmes, where listeners unwittingly excluded their greeting by reason of their choice of record. Clearly, one cannot repeat the same music too often. And if Mrs. X requests a tune that was played yesterday, she is going to be unlucky. I could hardly fail to notice that, after Sandy's broadcast to me, no one, but no one, had been even mildly interested in what he played. It was the hospital that counted. So I decided then and there, that, in my new programme, I myself would choose the records to go with the greetings, and, in this way, I could mention ten or a dozen names with each disc.

I have always tried to favour those whose need is perhaps the most pressing. First in the queue are the patients in hospital. They are shut away from home and loved ones. They are often extremely lonely, if not actually homesick. And, for them, a radio greeting can be of enormous benefit. Sometimes I have been criticised for favouring the hospitals in the north of Scotland. The truth is, I try to show no favouritism, but, on the other hand, where patients are in hospitals a long way from home, they do not have so many visitors. Some of them have no visitors at all. So I try to compensate for this situation, which is obviously more common in the remote places, than in the towns and cities of the south, where distances are not so great and visitors likely to be more plentiful.

Secondly, we like to remember the invalids at home. This category includes bed-ridden patients, partially bed-ridden patients, handicapped people, wheelchair invalids and blind people. Especially perhaps, blind people. It seems to me that in radio, more than in any other medium, we have such a wonderful opportunity for meeting blind people on their own ground. In radio, we are all sightless together. The listeners cannot see us. We cannot see them. For blind people, all the barriers are down. It is for this reason that I have encouraged people to write to me in braille over the years. Braille letters require no stamp, they are delivered by the Post Office without charge. They don't have the appearance of ordinary letters, being little rolls of stiff brown paper, on which the dots are embossed. I simply re-address the

ON MY WAVELENGTH

letters to May MacLachlan, who is blind and can type. She reads
the braille, types out the transcript, and sends it back to me. May
has been doing this for many years now. She has always taken
a keen interest in the programme, and is very good at telling me
when she thinks I am sounding cheerful — and also, when I'm not!
   The third group whom I tend to favour are the old people.
Why? Because it seems to me that, in the nature of things, the
old people are much more likely than young people to be house-
bound, and dependent on their radio. In any case, there is Radio
One, which is a non-stop programme for the young. I feel I should
try to redress the balance, however modestly, for the older
listeners. I try always to include some of the kind of music I
think they enjoy most. The old Scots songs, some Scottish dance
tunes, songs from the musicals of yesteryear, the light classics that
have stood the test of time. And, in general, I avoid what is
called 'pop' music in favour of the kind that older folk enjoy.
But not exclusively so. I had a letter once from an old person,
taking me to task for playing a mildly 'pop' record in the
programme. "We don't want that rubbish", she said dismissively.
I wrote back, saying I was sorry she hadn't liked it, but it was
really for a younger age group. "Young people get ill sometimes
too, you know", I said, "and young people have to go to hospital
sometimes. Is it not therefore reasonable to cater for their tastes?"
She wrote back at once, all contrition and apology. "You carry
on", she said, "you're doing fine!"
   When it comes to mentioning people's ages, or rather, **not**
mentioning them, I have a theory that one's age is a private matter.
There are, however, two age groups that like ages disclosed. They
are the very young and the very old. "I'm three and a half", says one
child. "I'm four and a quarter", says another. Note how they like
to add the fraction, to give them maturity. At the other end of
the scale are those of ninety and upwards. At that age, they **want**
their ages to be known. So we have a special group every week
of the nineties and upwards, and it is an unusual week, if we

129

don't have at least one of a hundred and over. I try to make a point of starting the programme with the children's greetings, if only because the young ones get impatient if they have to wait, and they may then spoil the show for their elders.

I have found the older listeners to be very responsive to the programme. Once, when I mentioned that I was going to be making an Appeal in the Week's Good Cause, on behalf of the Nurses' Benevolent Fund, a letter arrived, and, when I slit it open, out fluttered two single pound notes. The accompanying letter ran, "Dear Howard, Just to say thank you for all the pleasure you have given with your wonderful programme. Add the enclosed to your Appeal for the Nurses. A most worthy cause. O.A.P." No signature, just the revealing initials. I was very touched, not only by reason of the generous donation, but because O.A.P. chose to remain anonymous, wanting no thanks, no receipt. And taking me on trust. Thank you O.A.P.

The fourth and final group who have priority in my weekly broadcasts are the lonely people. Loneliness can hardly be peculiar to the twentieth century, but it does seem to be more prevalent. Or perhaps we are just more aware of it. First, there is the lonelieness of physical isolation. The people who live alone. These can be found in the remote places in the countryside, or in tenements or high flats in towns and cities. People deprived of company. For such as these, the radio is not only a source of entertainment and information, it is also a source of companionship. One listener wrote from Wester Ross saying, "I live alone, except for my budgie, Joey. I always answer you back when you say, "How are you to-day?" My nearest neighbour is five miles away. I get a visit from the postie when there is a letter, and the grocer's van comes once a week. I also get an occasional visit from the Minister, but I do not like it when he comes and your programme is on the air!" She then goes on to say she regards me as a friend who comes to visit her once a week.

And then there are those who are lonely by reason of temperament. People who find it difficult to communicate with their nearest and dearest. Such people often find it imperative to unburden themselves to someone. What they want is a sympathetic listener. Lucky are they, if they have a good friend or neighbour. If they haven't, they may go to a minister or priest. In extreme cases, they may go to a doctor or a psychiatrist. It may surprise you to know that we, in radio, often find ourselves cast in the role of listener. I think this is more common in radio than in television, simply because, as in the case of the blind, there is no vision. We can't see them. They can't see us. They build up a picture of what they think we look like from our voices, and they come to regard us as friends. After all, we are heard in their own homes. Our voices come to them in their own domestic surroundings. Not surprising then, that they come to a point where they want to write to us, as if they knew us. And don't forget it is often easier to unburden yourself to someone in writing, in a letter, than it would be in a face to face confrontation.

When people are kind enough to write me in appreciation of something I have done, I always try to write back and thank them. If they then write back and thank me for thanking them, I do not write back and thank them for thanking me for thanking them. If a situation develops, where they start writing to me frequently, I try to explain that I cannot enter into a regular correspondence. Even so, quite often a correspondence does develop, albeit a one-sided one on the part of the listener. I get regular letters from listeners, who may begin with a brief remark about the programme, but whose letters are mostly about their own limited interests and activities.

J. M. Barrie, in his fine little one-act play, 'The Old Lady Shows Her Medals', draws a poignant picture of an old woman who is so lonely that she invents an imaginary son. The play deals, in humour and pathos, with the consequences of her deception. Psychologically, he was right on the nail. There are those of such a temperament that, if they do not have someone as an object of their regard, they will invent a substitute. We, in radio, often find ourselves cast in this role. Hence the cards and little gifts that come to us at Christmas. The senders are often lonely souls who simply feel the need for someone to whom they can **give**.

Letters arriving at the BBC are left for me to collect, and this I do nearly every day. I bring them home, going through them in my office personally. I read every card and letter and file them in bundles. If a greeting is wanted to celebrate a birthday or an anniversary, I underline the date in red. When I come to build each week's programme, I consult the 'date' bundle first, in the hope of broadcasting the greeting on the nearest possible date. Hospital cards I mark with a double red cross, surely an appropriate symbol? In addition to requests for greetings, each week includes its quota of what we like to call 'fan mail'. These are letters, asking for nothing, just expressing enjoyment of the programme. And, quite often, the writers disclose domestic details about themselves. I regard these letters as private, although I always share with them our producer, Ben Lyons. Ben is the 'boss' behind the programme. He is responsible for it, as a member of BBC staff. He keeps me right, telling me how I sound — I have to guard against a tendency to sound 'sad' — and generally advising me on the content of the show. He and I have many a disagreement, but there has never been even one note of acrimony between us in all the years we have worked together. I always say, "I never fight with the producer. Unless I don't get my own way, of course!" Incidentally, Ben Lyons is not to be confused with the singular 'Lyon' from America, husband of the late and much-loved Bebe Daniels. Our Ben is a Scot. He and his efficient and helpful secretary, Jean Mackinnon, share any credit that may be attributed to the programme.

Although most of the people who write are women, we do get letters from men too. Some of the most regular and loyal fans are male. One old man wrote, "I have great difficulty in getting the kind of underwear I like. I like the kind that covers wrists, ankles and buttocks, can you help?" I had a good laugh at the question, but I found the information he wanted and sent it to him. Back came the reply, "You are a very friendly chap. I have ordered three sets. Steep at the price, but worth it in comfort". So if I've never achieved anything else in life, at least I've helped some old gentleman to comfort!

A woman wrote to me once, saying, "You have a very sympathetic voice. Will you please get my husband a job in the BBC?" I'm afraid I was not as sympathetic as she expected, especially as she went on to say he was a "very experienced pig and poultry keeper". I failed to see the connection. And then someone cruelly observed it was because of these 'corny programmes' I dish out!

And I confess to being somewhat nonplussed by the ambiguity of a recent card which simply said, "Your programme is such a tonic for everyone. Thank you for playing a record for my sister. She died the next day!" Looking back at this stage on the years of my career, I believe I can claim to be among the lucky ones. I have done so many of the things I wanted to do, and been paid for doing them! Naturally, I have enjoyed some of my activities more than others, as this account has no doubt disclosed. But, taking stock as things are at present, I am bound to admit that, of all the programmes and enterprises with which I have been connected over the years, I have had much the greatest satisfaction all round from my weekly greetings programme on BBC.

Exercising my imagination as I sit down in front of the mike, waiting for the cue to start, I never try to picture a large, anonymous mass of people. Rather, I try to focus my mind on one or two individuals, old people perhaps, or lonely ones, who are waiting too. On my wavelength. It is to them I address my opening greeting. "Hello (pause) How are you to-day?" (pause). And I wait. I always wait. So that I can hear the response — in my mind's ear. I like to think I can, in this way, perhaps, reach

HOWARD LOCKHART

out, and establish contact with some lonely soul. Certainly, on the
few occasions when I have, for devilment, omitted that first
salutation, someone has written in reproach, "And you never
asked us how we were last week!"

Recently a card ran, "When you say, 'how are you to-day?', I
nearly always say, 'Fine, thanks, Howard, how are you?' Unless
I'm in a bad mood. And then I say, 'None of your business!' ".

Which, come to think of it, is precisely as it should be . . .

INDEX

135

INDEX

INDEX

INDEX

139

Recommended Further Reading

'The Story of My Life'　　　　　　　　　　Helen Keller
　　　　　　　　　　　　　　　(Hodder & Stoughton)

'The Movies, Mr. Griffith and Me'　　　　　Lillian Gish
　　　　　　　　　　　　　　　　(W. H. Allen)

'Dancing in the Street'　　　　　　　　Clifford Hanley
　　　　　　　　　　　　　　　　(Hutchinson)

'Great Scot!' ('The Harry Lauder Story')　Gordon Irving
　　　　　　　　　　　　　　　(Leslie Frewin)

'Pavement in the Sun'　　　　　　　　　Jack House
　　　　　　　　　　　　　　　　(Hutchinson)